The little FRENCH cookbook

the little FRENCH cookbook

MURDOCH BOOKS
SYDNEY · LONDON

Contents

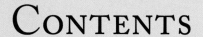

THE FRENCH PRESIDE OVER ONE OF THE WORLD'S
GREAT CULINARY HERITAGES AND NOWHERE
IS THAT HERITAGE MORE CELEBRATED, OR ENJOYED,
THAN IN FRANCE ITSELF.

France's reputation for wonderful food and cooking is often thought of as being based on technical skills and extravagant, expensive ingredients – on sauces that need to be reduced, and foie gras, truffles and other delicacies. This is haute cuisine, 'classic cooking', which was developed by the chefs of the French aristocracy and reached its heyday in the nineteenth century under legendary French chefs such as Auguste Escoffier.

Haute cuisine is a time-consuming art form that adheres to strict rules. This elegant form of cooking requires an understanding of its special methods and techniques, skills honed by long apprenticeships in the kitchens of the great restaurants, particularly in creating the subtle sauces that are its foundation. Nowadays this style of cooking is found mostly in expensive restaurants, but it can represent the highest art of cooking, one celebrated in stars by the famous Michelin guide.

Nouvelle cuisine, 'new cooking', was a reaction to the dominance of haute cuisine in the 1960s, when chefs, including Paul Bocuse and the Troisgros brothers, banded together to create lighter dishes, with less reliance on heavy sauces and a willingness to experiment with non-traditional ingredients and cooking styles. Nouvelle cuisine has encouraged innovation, and though some of its precepts were later abandoned, it had a lasting influence on French cooking.

Fundamentally, however, French food is a regionally based cuisine and many French dishes are named after their place of origin, from sole à la normande, to boeuf bourguignon. Eating your way around France the regional differences are still very distinct, and most restaurants cook not only the local dishes, but those of their own town or village. This is a result not only of tradition, but also of an enduring respect for local produce, the produits du terroir. Each area of France grows or produces food uniquely suited to its terrain and climate, from Bresse chickens to walnuts from Grenoble, butter from Normandy and mustard from Dijon. Today, there is more crossover between the provinces, and in markets, the best, not just the local, can be found, but the notion of regional specialities still underlies French cooking.

This respect for ingredients extends to only eating fruit and vegetables at the height of their season. Recipes change to reflect the best that each month has to offer, and every month, seasonal fruits and vegetables are eagerly awaited, from the summer melons of Provence to autumn walnuts and winter truffles in the Dordogne.

The French have gone to great lengths to protect their ingredients and traditional methods of food preparation. The *Appellation d'Origine Contrôlée* (AOC) system that they use to keep their cheeses and wines authentic is also being extended to an increasing number of important and regionally based food products, from Puy lentils to carrots from Créances.

The French love food and though many traditions have changed, and an office worker is just as likely to grab a sandwich on the run as enjoy a four-course lunch, as a foundation of French culture,

eating and drinking remain incredibly important. One of the great joys of France is starting the morning with a petit déjeuner of a fresh croissant and a café au lait. Lunch is still for many the main meal of the day, though dinner may be equally substantial, and with many shops and work places closed between 12:30 and 3:30, it can sometimes extend to three or four courses with wine.

Despite the emergence of the hypermarché, specialist food shops and weekly markets are an integral part of the French way of life. There is a boulangerie in every village; meat is purchased at a boucherie; while a charcuterie specialises in pork products and delicatessen items and a pâtisserie in baked goods. Markets are usually held weekly, and in some areas you can follow the same stallholders from town to town through the week. Even Paris has its neighbourhood markets, and there are also speciality markets, such as the garlic market in Aix-en-Provence in July and the foie gras market in the winter in Sarlat in Périgord.

THE FOOD OF THE NORTH
Paris is a world culinary centre, where local markets sell fantastic produce from all over France. Much of the city's reputation lies with its restaurants, a legacy of the revolution when private chefs had to find a new living. Parisians are discerning about their food and it is here you find the real home of the baguette, the country's most refined pâtisserie and finest cheese shops.

Brittany is traditionally a fishing and farming region with outstanding seafood, including native oysters, and wonderful early fruits and vegetables. Sweet crêpes and savoury buckwheat galettes are found throughout the region. Its sea salt, sel de Guérande, is used all over France.

Normandy is home to some of France's greatest cheeses: Camembert, Pont l'Evêque and Livarot; along with crème fraîche, butter and apples – three of the classic ingredients in French cuisine. There is also pré-salé lamb (lamb raised in salt marshes), mussels, oysters, cider and calvados.

Known as 'the Garden of France', the Loire Valley produces fruit, vegetables and white wines. Wild mushrooms are grown in the caves of Saumur and regional dishes include rillettes, andouillettes and tarte Tatin. The region also produces fine goat's cheeses, including Crottin de Chavignol. Poitou-Charentes on the Atlantic Coast has some of France's best oyster beds near Marennes, and is also home to Charentais melons, unsalted butter and Cognac.

Nord-Pas-de-Calais along the coast includes Boulogne-sur-mer, France's biggest fishing port. Inland are found the washed-rind Maroilles cheese, andouillettes and Flemish beers, used for cooking in dishes such as carbonnade à la flamande. Picardie has its vegetables, fruit and pré-salé lamb.

Champagne-Ardennes is a rural region, with Champagne being famous not just for its wine, but also for cheeses such as Brie and Chaource. In the North, the game forests of Ardennes have created a tradition of charcuterie. Their jambon d'Ardennes and pâtés d'Ardennes are famous around the world.

Bordering Germany, Alsace-Lorraine's heritage is reflected in its cuisine. Its charcuterie is used in quiche lorraine, choucroute garnie, tarte flambée and baeckenoffe (stew). Meat dishes à la lorraine are served with red cabbage cooked in wine, while Alsace's baking has Germanic influences, with pretzels, rye bread and kugelhopf.

THE FOOD OF THE EAST AND CENTRE

Central France is made up of the regions of Auvergne and Limousin. With very cold winters, the cuisine of these areas tends to be hearty and potatoes and cabbages are heavily used for dishes such as aligot and potée auvergnate (one-pot pork and cabbage stew). Limousin is famous for its beef, lamb, pork and veal and Auvergne for its game and tiny green Puy lentils. The area also produces Cantal and Saint Nectaire cheeses, as well as blue cheeses such as Bleu d'Auvergne and Fourme d'Ambert. Auvergne is known for its bottled mineral waters, including Vichy and Volvic.

Burgundy is world-famous for its red and white wines with the wine industry centred around the town of Beaune. Burgundian dishes tend to be rich, full of flavour and a perfect match for the area's wines. Wine is also an important part of the region's cooking, and à la bourguignonne usually means cooked in red wine. Boeuf bourguignon, coq au vin, Bresse chicken cooked with cream and wild morels, snails filled with garlic herb butter and slices of jambon persillé (ham and parsley in aspic) are Burgundian classics. Dijon is synonymous with mustard and is also the home of pain d'épices (spicy gingerbread) and kir, made of white wine and crème de cassis from local blackcurrants.

Red wine is used in cooking and dishes in which it is included are usually known as à la bordelaise.

One of France's great gastronomic capitals, Lyon is home to great restaurants, including Paul Bocuse's, as well as many simple bouchons (traditionally working-class cafés) and brasseries all over the city. Considered to be the charcuterie centre of France, Lyon is renowned for andouillettes, cervelas and rosette sausages, served at bouchons along with salade lyonnaise, pike quenelles, poulet au vinaigre (chicken stewed in vinegar), potato gratins, the fresh herb cheese, cervelle de canut (silk-weavers' brains) and bottles of local Beaujolais or Côtes du Rhône. The surrounding countryside produces excellent fruit and vegetables, as well as AOC chickens from Bourg-en-Bresse.

The East of France rises up into the French Alps and is made up of three regions, Franche-Comté in the North and Savoie and Dauphiné in the South. These mountain regions have great cheesemaking traditions and in the summer, alpages cheeses such as Reblochon are still made from animals that are taken up to the high meadows. Tomme de Savoie, Beaufort and Comté are other mountain cheeses and dishes include fondues and raclettes. Potatoes are found all over the Centre and the East, but it is Dauphiné that gives its name to the famous gratin dauphinois.

THE FOOD OF THE SOUTH AND SOUTHWEST

Bordeaux is associated with great wines and the grands crus of Médoc and Saint Emilion are world-famous, as are dessert wines from Sauternes. Red wine is used in cooking and dishes in which it is included are usually known as à la bordelaise, such as entrecôte à la bordelaise. Oysters from the Atlantic beds at Arcachon and pré-salé lamb from Pauillac are specialities of the area.

Goose and duck confit and foie gras are the Dordogne and Lot's most famous exports along with the black truffles and walnuts of Périgord. Black truffles and foie gras are used as a garnish in many Southwest dishes and these dishes are sometimes known as à la périgourdine. Walnuts are used in salade aux noix and to flavour oils, and prunes are grown at Agen.

Gascony is a rural area that produces Armagnac and is famous, along with the Dordogne, for its foie gras, duck and goose confit, pâtés and terrines and for the use of goose fat in its cooking. Home-made and local specialities can be tasted at fermes auberges (farmhouse restaurants).

The Southwest Basque country close to Spain flavours its food with spicy piment d'Espelette, dried chillies, which are also often used in the salting mixture for the local Bayonne ham. Tuna are caught off the Atlantic coast. The tradition of baking, such as making gâteau basque, is strong.

The flavours of Provence are the flavours of the Mediterranean: olives, olive oil, garlic, eggplants (aubergines), zucchini (courgettes), tomatoes and herbes de provence, along with peaches, melons from Cavaillon and strawberries. Provençal cuisine includes the strong flavours of aïoli, anchoïade and tapenade; pissaladière and pistou from the Italian-bordering Côte d'Azur; simple grilled fish and the classic bouillabaisse; red rice from the Camargue and honey and candied fruit.

Chapter 1

SOUPS

∞∞∞∞∞∞∞∞∞∞∞∞∞∞∞∞∞∞∞∞∞∞∞∞∞∞∞∞∞∞∞∞∞∞

Soups make the most of plentiful seasonal and regional produce, and can be a meal in themselves. Aromatic herbs and spices are used to complement the robust flavours of seafood, poultry and vegetables.

BOURRIDE
Provençale Fish Soup with Garlic Mayonnaise

This rich fish soup can be served in a variety of ways. The bread can be put in a dish with the fish piled on top and the soup ladled over, or the broth may be served with croutons and the fish eaten separately with boiled potatoes as a main course.

GARLIC CROUTONS
½ stale baguette, sliced
60 ml (2 fl oz/¼ cup) olive oil
1 garlic clove, halved

AIOLI
2 egg yolks
4 garlic cloves, crushed
3–5 teaspoons lemon juice
250 ml (9 fl oz/1 cup) olive oil

¼ teaspoon saffron threads
1 litre (35 fl oz/4 cups) dry white wine

1 leek, white part only, chopped
2 carrots, chopped
2 onions, chopped
2 long pieces orange zest
2 teaspoons fennel seeds
3 sprigs of thyme
2.5 kg (5 lb 10 oz) whole firm white fish such as
    monkfish, sea bass, cod, perch, sole or bream,
    filleted, skinned and cut into 4 cm (1½ in) pieces
    (reserve the trimmings)
3 egg yolks

To make the garlic croutons, preheat the oven to 160°C (315°F/Gas 2–3). Brush the bread with oil and bake for 10 minutes, or until crisp. Rub one side of each slice with garlic.

To make the aïoli, put the egg yolks, garlic and 3 teaspoons lemon juice in a mortar and pestle or food processor and pound or mix until light and creamy. Add the oil, drop by drop from the tip of a teaspoon, whisking constantly until it begins to thicken, then add the oil in a very thin stream. (If using a food processor, pour in the oil in a thin stream with the motor running.) Season, add the remaining lemon juice and, if necessary, thin with a little warm water. Cover and refrigerate.

Soak the saffron in 1 tablespoon of hot water for 15 minutes. Put the saffron and soaking liquid in a large saucepan with the wine, leek, carrot, onion, orange zest, fennel seeds, thyme, fish trimmings and 1 litre (35 fl oz/4 cups) water. Cover and bring to the boil, then simmer for 20 minutes, skimming occasionally. Strain into a clean saucepan, pressing the solids with a wooden spoon to extract all the liquid. Bring the stock to a gentle simmer, add half the fish pieces and poach for 5 minutes. Remove and keep warm while you cook the rest of the fish, then remove all of the fish from the pan and bring the stock back to the boil. Boil for 5 minutes, or until slightly reduced, then remove from the heat.

Put half the aïoli and the egg yolks in a bowl and mix until smooth. Whisk in a ladleful of hot stock, then gradually add 5 ladlefuls, stirring constantly. Pour back into the pan holding the rest of the stock and whisk over low heat for 3–5 minutes, or until the soup is hot and slightly thicker (don't let it boil or it will curdle). Season to taste.

To serve, put two garlic croutons in each bowl, top with a few pieces of the fish and ladle over the hot soup. Serve the remaining aïoli separately.

SERVES 4

BISQUE DE CRABE

Crab Bisque

Originally, bisques were made with poultry and game birds (in particular pigeons) and were more of a stew. Today, they have evolved into rich velvety soups and tend to use crustaceans. You can reserve some of the crabmeat or claws for a garnish.

1 kg (2 lb 4 oz) live crabs
50 g (2 oz) butter
½ carrot, finely chopped
½ onion, finely chopped
1 celery stalk, finely chopped
1 bay leaf
2 sprigs of thyme

2 tablespoons tomato paste (concentrated purée)
2 tablespoons brandy
150 ml (5 fl oz) dry white wine
1 litre (35 fl oz/4 cups) fish stock
60 g (2 oz) rice
60 ml (2 fl oz/¼ cup) thick (double/heavy) cream
¼ teaspoon cayenne pepper

Put the crabs in the freezer for 1 hour. Remove the top shell and bony tail flap from the underside of each crab. Remove the gills from both sides of the crab and the grit sac. Detach the claws and legs.

Heat the butter in a large saucepan and add the vegetables, bay leaf and thyme. Cook over moderate heat for 3 minutes, without allowing the vegetables to colour. Add the crab claws, legs and body and cook for 5 minutes, or until the shells turn red. Add the tomato paste, brandy and wine and simmer for 2 minutes, or until reduced by half.

Add the stock and 500 ml (17 fl oz/2 cups) water and bring to the boil. Reduce the heat and simmer

for 5 minutes. Remove the shells and reserve the claws. Finely crush the shells with a pestle and mortar (or in a food processor with a little of the soup). Return the crushed shells to the soup with the rice. Bring to the boil, then reduce the heat and simmer, covered, for 30 minutes, or until the rice is very soft.

Strain the bisque into a clean saucepan through a fine sieve lined with damp muslin, pressing firmly on the solids to extract all the cooking liquid. Add the cream and season with salt and cayenne, then gently reheat to serve. Ladle into warmed soup bowls and garnish, if you like, with the crab claws or some of the meat.

SERVES 4

Right: Detach the claws and legs from each crab.

Far right: Add the tomato paste, brandy and wine to the crab mixture and simmer until reduced.

Soupe à l'ail

Garlic Soup

Garlic soups are served throughout France. In Provence, a simple soup of garlic, herbs and olive oil is known as aïgo bouïdo. The Southwest version, made with goose fat, is called le tourin. This soup is given more substance with potato to thicken it.

2 bulbs of garlic, about 30 cloves, cloves separated
125 ml (4 fl oz/½ cup) olive oil
125 g (5 oz) streaky bacon, finely chopped
1 floury potato, diced
1.5 litres (52 fl oz/6 cups) chicken stock or water
bouquet garni
3 egg yolks

CHEESE CROUTONS
½ baguette or 1 ficelle, sliced
40 g (1½ oz/¼ cup) grated Gruyère cheese

Smash the garlic with the flat side of a knife and peel. Heat 1 tablespoon of the oil in a large heavy-based saucepan and cook the bacon over moderate heat for 5 minutes, without browning. Add the garlic and potato and cook for 5 minutes, or until softened. Add the stock and bouquet garni, bring to the boil and then simmer for 30 minutes, or until the potato starts to dissolve into the soup.

Put the egg yolks in a large bowl and pour in the remaining olive oil in a thin stream, whisking until thickened. Gradually whisk in the hot soup. Strain back into the saucepan, pressing to extract all the liquid, and heat gently without boiling. Season.

To make the cheese croutons, preheat the grill (broiler) and lightly toast the bread on both sides. Sprinkle with the cheese and grill (broil) until melted. Place a few croutons in each warm bowl and ladle the soup over the top.

SERVES 4

Far left: Smash the garlic cloves with the flat side of a knife to loosen the skin.

Left: Keeping the garlic cloves whole, rather than chopping them, gives a much sweeter flavour.

Soupe à l'oignon gratinée
French Onion Soup

50 g (2 oz) butter
750 g (1 lb 11 oz) onions, thinly sliced
2 garlic cloves, finely chopped
40 g (1½ oz/⅓ cup) plain (all-purpose) flour
2 litres (70 fl oz/8 cups) beef or chicken stock

250 ml (9 fl oz/1 cup) white wine
1 bay leaf
2 sprigs of thyme
12 slices stale baguette
100 g (4 oz/¾ cup) finely grated Gruyère cheese

Melt the butter in a heavy-based saucepan over low heat. Add the onion slices and cook, stirring occasionally, for 25 minutes, or until the onion is deep golden brown and beginning to caramelise. Add the garlic and flour and stir constantly for 2 minutes.

Gradually blend in the stock and the wine, stirring all the time, and bring to the boil. Add the bay leaf and thyme and season. Cover the pan and simmer for 25 minutes. Remove the bay leaf and thyme and check the seasoning.

Preheat the grill (broiler). Toast the baguette slices, then divide among six warm soup bowls and ladle the soup over the top. Sprinkle with the cheese and grill (broil) until the cheese melts and turns light golden brown. Serve immediately.

PICTURE ON PAGE 22

SERVES 6

Potage poireaux-pommes de terre
Leek and Potato Soup

50 g (2 oz) butter
1 onion, finely chopped
3 leeks, white part only, sliced
1 celery stalk, finely chopped
1 garlic clove, finely chopped

200 g (7 oz) potatoes, chopped
750 ml (27 fl oz/3 cups) chicken stock
185 ml (6 fl oz/¾ cup) cream
2 tablespoons chopped chives

Melt the butter in a large saucepan and add the onion, leek, celery and garlic. Cover and cook over low heat, stirring occasionally, for 15 minutes, or until the vegetables are softened but not browned. Add the potato and stock and bring to the boil. Reduce the heat and leave to simmer, covered, for 20 minutes.

Allow the soup to cool a little before puréeing in a blender or food processor.

Return the soup to the clean saucepan and gently return to the boil. Stir in the cream, season with salt and white pepper and reheat without boiling. Serve hot or well chilled, garnished with chives.

SERVES 6

Consommé de poulet
Chicken Consommé

STOCK
1 kg (2 lb 4 oz) chicken carcasses, halved
200 g (7 oz) chicken legs
1 carrot, chopped
1 onion, chopped
1 celery stalk, chopped
2 sprigs of parsley
20 black peppercorns
1 bay leaf
1 sprig of thyme

CLARIFICATION MIXTURE
2 chicken legs
1 carrot, finely chopped

1 leek, finely chopped
1 celery stalk, finely chopped
2 tomatoes, chopped
10 black peppercorns
1 sprig of parsley, chopped
2 egg whites, lightly beaten
sea salt

1 small carrot, julienned
1/2 small leek, white part only, julienned

To make the stock, remove and discard any skin and fat from the chicken carcasses and legs. Place in a large heavy-based saucepan and add 3 litres (105 fl oz/12 cups) cold water. Bring to the boil and skim the fat that rises to the surface. Add the remaining ingredients to the pan and simmer for 1 1/2 hours, skimming occasionally. Strain the stock to give about 1.5 litres (52 fl oz/6 cups) and return it to the clean saucepan.

To make the clarification mixture, discard the skin from the chicken legs. Remove the meat and chop it finely (you will need about 150 g/6 oz) and mix with the carrot, leek, celery, tomato, peppercorns, parsley and egg white. Add 185 ml (6 fl oz/3/4 cup) of the warm stock to loosen the mixture.

Add the clarification mixture to the strained stock and whisk in well. Bring to a gentle simmer. As the mixture simmers the clarification ingredients will bind with any impurities and form a 'raft'. As the raft rises, gently move it with a wooden spoon to one side of the saucepan away from the main movement of the simmering stock (this will make it easier to ladle out the stock later). Simmer for 1 hour, or until the stock is clear.

Ladle out the stock, taking care not to disturb the raft, and strain it through a fine sieve lined with damp muslin. Place sheets of paper towel over the top of the consommé and then quickly lift away to remove any remaining fat. Season with coarse sea salt (or use other iodine-free salt, as iodine will cloud the soup).

Just before serving, reheat the consommé. Put the julienned vegetables in a saucepan of boiling water and cook for 2 minutes, or until just tender. Drain well, spoon into warmed soup bowls and pour the consommé over the top.

SERVES 4

Chapter 2

HORS D'OEUVRES

∞∞∞∞∞∞∞∞∞∞∞∞∞∞∞∞∞∞∞∞∞∞∞∞∞∞∞∞∞∞

From toasted bread with flavoursome toppings to elegant and simple fingerfood, hors d'oeuvres are a light beginning to a meal or ideal food for a party.

PETITS FARCIS
Provençale Stuffed Vegetables

This wonderful dish from Provence makes good use of the region's abundance of garden produce and the stuffing can include any herbs, meat or cheeses at hand. Serve hot or cold with bread for a simple summer lunch.

2 small eggplants (aubergines), halved lengthways
2 small zucchini (courgettes), halved lengthways
4 tomatoes
2 small red capsicums (peppers), halved lengthways
    and seeded
4 tablespoons olive oil
2 red onions, chopped
2 garlic cloves, crushed

250 g (9 oz) minced (ground) pork
250 g (9 oz) minced (ground) veal
50 g (2 oz) tomato paste (concentrated purée)
80 ml (3 fl oz/⅓ cup) white wine
2 tablespoons chopped parsley
50 g (2 oz/½ cup) grated Parmesan cheese
80 g (3 oz/1 cup) fresh breadcrumbs

Preheat the oven to 180°C (350°F/Gas 4). Grease a large roasting tin with oil. Using a spoon, hollow out the eggplants and zucchini, leaving a border around the edge. Finely chop the flesh. Slice the tops off the tomatoes (don't throw away the tops). Using a spoon to hollow out the centres, catching the juice in a bowl, and roughly chop the flesh. Arrange the vegetables, including the capsicum, in the tin. Brush the edges of the eggplants and zucchini with a little of the olive oil. Pour 125 ml (4 fl oz/½ cup) water into the tin.

Heat half the oil in a large frying pan. Cook the onion and garlic for 3 minutes, or until softened.

Add the pork and veal and stir for 5 minutes until the meat browns, breaking up any lumps with the back of a fork. Add the finely chopped eggplant and zucchini and cook for another 3 minutes. Add the tomato pulp and juice, tomato paste and wine. Cook, stirring occasionally, for 10 minutes.

Remove the pan from the heat. Stir in the parsley, Parmesan and breadcrumbs. Season well with salt and pepper. Spoon the mixture into the vegetables. Place the tops back on the tomatoes. Sprinkle the vegetables with the remaining olive oil and bake for 45 minutes, or until the vegetables are tender.

SERVES 4

Far left: Hollow out the vegetables with a spoon and brush the edges with a little oil.

Left: Carefully fill the vegetables with the meat stuffing.

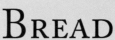

BREAD

✧✧✧

Bread is an essential part of French life. Eaten with every meal, bread is bought daily, or even twice daily, and by law, every village in France must have a shop making or selling bread.

Breads are sold not only by the loaf (la pièce) but also by weight, perpetuating the tradition of buying just enough bread for each meal or day. Boulangeries bake twice daily so that people can have the freshest bread possible, especially since a baguette made of just wheat flour, yeast and salt begins to go stale after only a few hours.

Bread has been the staple of the French diet since the Middle Ages. The first loaves were large and coarse, made from a mix of flours and unsalted because of the high price of salt. It was not until the seventeenth century that white bread was invented when a method for removing bran was discovered.

The baguette is considered a symbol of France, but many French people see it instead as a symbol of Paris. Invented in the nineteenth century and based on Viennese bread, it was made from white flour and a sourdough starter, rolled up into a slim, light loaf with lots of crust. Paris, always a great consumer of bread due to its position in the centre of the Beauce wheat plains, immediately took to the new loaf, though it was not until the twentieth century that it became popular in rural France. The best baguettes have a crisp, golden outside, with the score marks rising above the crust.

Although the elegant baguette is France's most popular bread, the more rustic and nutritious pain de campagne is growing in popularity, as are other loaves made from barley and rye. These country-style breads often use a levain (sourdough starter) rather than yeast. Sourdough breads have a long production time, but they do keep for a few days rather than going stale quickly like baguettes. These loaves may also be baked in a wood-fired oven, which adds a smoky taste.

A real baguette is a certain weight and size, about 70 cm (28 in) in length and 250 g (9 oz) in weight. Not all long loaves are baguettes. A flûte is heavier and longer, and a ficelle thinner and lighter, though all are made in the same way. A long, thin pain au levain (sourdough bread) may also be labelled as a baguette, as the shape is now so recognizable that the name covers many things.

GOUGÈRES À LA TRUITE FUMÉE
Smoked Trout Gougère

80 g (3 oz) butter
125 g (5 oz/1 cup) plain (all-purpose) flour, sifted twice
¼ teaspoon paprika
3 large eggs, beaten
100 g (4 oz/¾ cup) grated Gruyère cheese

FILLING
400 g (14 oz) smoked trout
100 g (4 oz) watercress, trimmed
30 g (1 oz) butter
1 tablespoon plain (all-purpose) flour
300 ml (11 fl oz) milk

Preheat the oven to 200°C (400°F/Gas 6) and put a baking tray on the top shelf to heat up. Lightly grease a shallow baking dish.

Melt the butter with 185 ml (6 fl oz/¾ cup) water in a saucepan. Bring the mixture to a rolling boil, then remove from the heat and sift in all the flour and the paprika. Return the pan to the heat and beat continuously with a wooden spoon to make a smooth shiny paste that comes away from the side of the pan. Cool for a few minutes.

Beat the eggs into the mixture, one at a time, until it is shiny and smooth – the dough should drop off the spoon but not be too runny. Stir in two-thirds of the cheese.

Spoon the dough around the edge of the prepared dish. Put this in the oven on the hot tray and cook for 45–50 minutes, or until well risen and browned.

Meanwhile, to make the filling, peel the skin off the trout, lift off the top fillet and then pull out the bone. Break the trout into large flakes.

Wash the watercress and put in a large saucepan with just the water clinging to the leaves. Cover and steam for 2 minutes, or until the watercress is just wilted. Drain, cool and squeeze out the liquid with your hands. Roughly chop the watercress.

Melt the butter in a saucepan, stir in the flour to make a roux and cook, stirring, for 3 minutes over very low heat without allowing the roux to brown. Remove from the heat and add the milk gradually, stirring after each addition until smooth. Return to the heat and simmer for 3 minutes. Stir in the smoked trout and watercress and season well.

Spoon the filling into the centre of the pastry shell and bake for 10 minutes. Serve immediately.

SERVES 4

Spoon the choux pastry around the edge of the baking dish and bake until well risen.

Millefeuille aux poireaux et oeufs pochés

Millefeuille of Leeks and Poached Eggs

Millefeuille means 'a thousand leaves' and refers to the many layers of the puff pastry. You can either use the recipe in this book or use 350 g (12 oz) of ready-made puff pastry. Make sure you use the freshest eggs you can find.

½ quantity puff pastry (page 180)
1 egg, lightly beaten
30 g (1 oz) butter
3 leeks, white part only, cut into julienne strips
4 eggs

BEURRE BLANC
2 French shallots, finely chopped
1 tablespoon butter
3 tablespoons white wine
185 ml (6 fl oz/¾ cup) chicken stock
175 g (6 oz) unsalted butter, chilled and diced

Preheat the oven to 190°C (375°F/Gas 5). Roll out the pastry on a lightly floured surface to a 24 x 12 cm (9½ x 5 in) rectangle. Chill for 10 minutes, then cut into four triangles. Place on a damp baking tray, lightly brush with the beaten egg and bake for 15 minutes, or until puffed and golden brown. Slice the triangles in half horizontally and use a spoon to remove any uncooked dough from the inside.

Melt the butter in a frying pan, add the leek and cook, stirring, for 10 minutes, or until the leek is tender. Season with salt.

Bring a pan of water to the boil. Crack an egg into a ramekin, then reduce the heat and slide the egg into the simmering water. Poach for 3 minutes,

remove carefully with a slotted spoon and drain on paper towels. Poach all the eggs in the same way.

To make the beurre blanc, gently fry the shallots in the butter until tender but not brown. Pour in the wine and boil until reduced by half. Add the stock and cook until reduced by a third, then add the butter, piece by piece, whisking continuously until the sauce thickens and taking care not to overheat. Season with salt and white pepper.

Arrange the base triangles of pastry on a serving dish, top each one with a spoonful of warm leek, then a poached egg and a little beurre blanc. Cover with the pastry tops and serve with the rest of the beurre blanc drizzled around or on the side.

SERVES 4

When making the beurre blanc, take care not to overheat the sauce or the butter will melt too quickly and not form an emulsion.

Pissaladière

Onion and Anchovy Tart

Pissaladière takes its name from pissalat, puréed anchovies. It can vary in its topping from onions and anchovies to onions, tomatoes and anchovies or simply anchovies puréed with garlic. Traditional to Nice, it can be made with a bread or pastry base.

40 g (1 ½ oz) butter
2 tablespoons olive oil
1.5 kg (3 lb 6 oz) onions, thinly sliced
2 tablespoons thyme leaves

1 quantity bread dough (page 176)
16 anchovies, halved lengthways
24 pitted olives

Melt the butter with half the oil in a saucepan and add the onion and half the thyme. Cover and cook over low heat, stirring occasionally, for 45 minutes, or until the onion is softened but not browned. Season and set aside to cool.

Preheat the oven to 200°C (400°F/Gas 6). Roll out the bread dough to roughly fit an oiled 34 x 26 cm (13½ x 10½ in) shallow baking tray. Brush with the remaining oil, then spread with the onion.

Lay the anchovies in a lattice pattern over the top of the onion and arrange the olives in the lattice diamonds. Bake for 20 minutes, or until the dough is cooked and lightly browned. Sprinkle with the remaining thyme leaves and cut into squares. Serve hot or warm.

SERVES 6

Right: Spread the softened onion over the bread base.

Far right: Arrange the anchovies over the top in the traditional lattice pattern.

Escargots à la bourguignonne
Snails with Garlic Butter

There are many varieties of edible snails, with the most common being petits gris or the slightly larger escargots de Bourgogne, also known as the Roman snail. Canned snails are sold along with their shells and are easier to use than fresh ones.

250 ml (9 fl oz/1 cup) white wine
250 ml (9 fl oz/1 cup) chicken stock
3 sprigs of tarragon
24 canned snails, well drained
24 snail shells

2 garlic cloves, crushed
2 tablespoons finely chopped basil leaves
2 tablespoons finely chopped parsley
2 tablespoons finely chopped tarragon leaves
150 g (6 oz) butter, at room temperature

Put the wine, chicken stock, tarragon and 125 ml (4 fl oz/½ cup) water in a small saucepan and boil for 2 minutes. Add the snails, reduce the heat and simmer for 7 minutes. Leave to cool in the liquid. Drain and place a snail in each shell. Preheat the oven to 200°C (400°F/Gas 6).

Mix together the garlic, basil, parsley, tarragon and butter and season well. Put a little garlic butter in each shell and arrange on a snail plate or baking tray covered with rock salt. Bake for 7–8 minutes, or until the butter melts and the snails are heated through. Serve immediately with crusty bread.

SERVES 4

Rémoulade de céleri-rave
Celeriac Remoulade

MUSTARD MAYONNAISE
2 egg yolks
1 tablespoon white wine vinegar
1 tablespoon Dijon mustard
125 ml (4 fl oz/½ cup) light olive oil

juice of 1 lemon
2 celeriac, trimmed and peeled
2 tablespoons capers
5 cornichons, chopped
2 tablespoons finely chopped parsley

To make the mayonnaise, whisk together the yolks, vinegar and mustard in a bowl or food processor. Add the oil, drop by drop from the tip of a spoon, whisking until it begins to thicken, then add the oil in a thin stream. (If you're using a processor, add the oil in a thin stream with the motor running.) Season. If necessary, thin with a little warm water.

Place 1 litre (35 fl oz/4 cups) water in a bowl with half the lemon juice. Grate the celeriac and add to the bowl. Bring a pan of water to the boil. Add the remaining lemon juice. Drain the celeriac and add to the pan for 1 minute, then drain and cool under running water. Pat dry with paper towels and toss with the mayonnaise, capers, cornichons and parsley.

SERVES 6

Huîtres Mornay
Oysters Mornay

24 oysters in their shells
50 g (2 oz) butter
1 French shallot, finely chopped
30 g (1 oz/¼ cup) plain (all-purpose) flour
375 ml (13 fl oz/1½ cups) milk

pinch of nutmeg
½ bay leaf
35 g (1 oz/¼ cup) grated Gruyère cheese
25 g (1 oz/¼ cup) grated Parmesan cheese,
   plus a little extra for grilling (broiling)

Shuck the oysters, reserving the liquid. Strain the liquid into a saucepan. Rinse the oysters to remove any bits of shell. Wash and dry the shells.

Melt 30 g (1 oz) of the butter in a saucepan, add the shallot and cook, stirring, for 3 minutes. Stir in the flour to make a roux and stir over very low heat for 3 minutes without allowing the roux to brown. Remove from the heat and gradually add the milk, stirring after each addition until smooth. Return to the heat, add the nutmeg and bay leaf and simmer for 5 minutes. Strain through a fine sieve into a clean pan.

Heat the oyster liquid in the saucepan to a simmer (add a little water if you need some more liquid). Add the oysters and poach for 30 seconds, then lift them out with a slotted spoon and return them to their shells. Stir the cooking liquid into the sauce. Add the cheeses and the remaining butter and stir until they have melted into the sauce. Season with salt and pepper.

Preheat the grill (broiler). Spoon a little sauce over each oyster, sprinkle with the Parmesan and place under the grill (broiler) for a couple of minutes, or until golden.

SERVES 4

To store oysters, wrap them in a damp cloth and refrigerate in the salad compartment for up to 3 days. Eat oysters that have been shucked immediately.

Chapter 3

EGGS AND CHEESE

*The French are the masters of cooking with eggs and cheese.
Whether it be whisking egg whites to make light-as-air soufflés,
folding eggs for a delicious creamy omelette or combining local
eggs and cheese to create a delicious blue cheese quiche.*

SOUFFLÉ DE COURGETTES

Zucchini Soufflé

Soufflés have developed a reputation as unpredictable creations, but they are not hard to make. The secret lies in beating the egg whites to the right stiffness and serving the soufflé straight from the oven. You can use broccoli instead of zucchini in this recipe.

1 tablespoon butter, melted
1 1/2 tablespoons dried breadcrumbs
350 g (12 oz) zucchini (courgettes), chopped
125 ml (4 fl oz/1/2 cup) milk
30 g (1 oz) butter

30 g (1 oz/1/4 cup) plain (all-purpose) flour
85 g (3 oz) Gruyère or Parmesan cheese, finely grated
3 spring onions (scallions), finely chopped
4 eggs, separated

Brush a 1.5 litre (52 fl oz/6 cup) soufflé dish with the melted butter. Tip the breadcrumbs into the dish, then rotate the dish to coat the side with breadcrumbs. Tip out the excess breadcrumbs.

Cook the zucchini in a saucepan of boiling water for 8 minutes, or until tender. Drain and transfer to a food processor. Add the milk and mix until smooth. Alternatively, mash the zucchini with the milk, then press it through a sieve with a wooden spoon. Preheat the oven to 180°C (350°F/Gas 4).

Melt the butter in a saucepan over low heat and stir in the flour to make a roux. Cook, stirring, for 2 minutes without allowing the roux to brown. Remove from the heat and add the zucchini purée, stirring until smooth. Return the pan to the heat and bring to the boil. Reduce the heat and simmer, stirring, for 3 minutes, then remove from the heat. Pour into a bowl, add the cheese and spring onion and season well. Mix until smooth, then beat in the egg yolks until smooth again.

Whisk the egg whites in a clean dry bowl until they form soft peaks. Spoon a quarter of the egg white onto the zucchini mixture and quickly but lightly fold it in, to loosen the mixture. Lightly fold in the remaining egg white. Pour the mixture into the soufflé dish. Run your thumb around the rim of the dish, about 2 cm (3/4 in) into the soufflé mixture (try not to wipe off the breadcrumbs and butter). This helps the soufflé rise without sticking.

Bake for 45 minutes, or until the soufflé is well risen and wobbles slightly when tapped. Test with a metal skewer through a crack in the side of the soufflé – the skewer should come out either clean or slightly moist. If the skewer is slightly moist, by the time the soufflé makes it to the table it will be cooked in the centre. Serve immediately.

SERVES 4

Pipérade

Basque Omelette

This traditional Basque dish is a delicious melding of ratatouille and eggs. The name is derived from 'piper', meaning red pepper in the local dialect. The eggs can either be cooked more like an omelette or scrambled together as done here.

2 tablespoons olive oil
1 large onion, thinly sliced
2 red capsicums (peppers), seeded and cut into batons
2 garlic cloves, crushed
750 g (1 lb 11 oz) tomatoes

pinch of cayenne pepper
8 eggs, lightly beaten
2 teaspoons butter
4 thin slices of ham, such as Bayonne

Heat the oil in a large heavy-based frying pan. Cook the onion for 3 minutes, or until softened. Add the capsicum and garlic, cover and cook for 8 minutes to soften – stir frequently and don't allow it to brown.

Score a cross in the top of each tomato. Plunge them into boiling water for 20 seconds, then drain and peel the skin away from the cross. Chop the tomatoes, discarding the cores. Spoon the tomato and cayenne over the capsicum, cover the pan and cook for a further 5 minutes.

Uncover the pan and increase the heat. Cook for 3 minutes, or until all the juices have evaporated, shaking the pan often. Season well with salt and pepper. Add the beaten eggs and scramble into the mixture until they are cooked.

Heat the butter in a small frying pan and fry the ham. Arrange on the pipérade and serve at once.

SERVES 4

Right: Spoon the chopped tomato over the onion and capsicum.

Far right: Add the egg and scramble lightly, remembering that it will continue to cook after it is removed from the heat.

CERVELLE DE CANUT
Fresh Cheese with Herbs

Cervelle de canut is a Lyonnais dish. The name means 'silk weavers' brains' (apparently silk weavers were considered to be quite stupid). Depending on the type of cheese that you use, the dish can be smooth and creamy or more coarse.

500 g (1 lb 2 oz) fromage blanc or curd cheese
2 tablespoons olive oil
1 garlic clove, finely chopped
2 tablespoons chopped chervil

4 tablespoons chopped parsley
2 tablespoons chopped chives
1 tablespoon chopped tarragon
4 French shallots, finely chopped

Beat the fromage blanc or curd cheese with a wooden spoon, then add the olive oil and garlic and beat it into the cheese. Add the herbs and shallots and mix together well.

Season and serve with pieces of toast or bread, perhaps after dessert as you would serve cheese and biscuits.

SERVES 8

QUICHE AU BLEU
Blue Cheese Quiche

100 g (4 oz/1 cup) walnuts
1 quantity tart pastry (page 178)
200 g (7 oz) blue cheese, mashed
80 ml (3 fl oz/⅓ cup) milk

3 eggs
2 egg yolks
185 ml (6 fl oz/¾ cup) thick (double/heavy) cream

Preheat the oven to 200°C (400°F/Gas 6). Toast the walnuts on a baking tray for 5 minutes, then cool and chop.

Line a 25 cm (10 in) fluted loose-based tart tin with the tart pastry. Line the pastry shell with a crumpled piece of greaseproof paper and baking beads (use dried beans or rice if you don't have baking beads). Blind bake the pastry shell for 10 minutes, then remove the paper and beads.

Bake for another 3–5 minutes, or until the pastry is just cooked but still very pale. Reduce the oven to 180°C (350°F/Gas 4).

Mix together the blue cheese, milk, eggs, egg yolks and cream and season with salt and pepper. Pour into the pastry shell and scatter with the walnuts. Bake for 25–30 minutes, or until the filling is just set. Leave in the tin for 5 minutes before serving.

SERVES 8

Oeufs en cocotte
Baked Eggs

1 tablespoon butter, melted
125 ml (4 fl oz/½ cup) thick (double/heavy) cream
4 button mushrooms, finely chopped
40 g (1½ oz) ham, finely chopped

40 g (1½ oz) Gruyère cheese, finely chopped
4 eggs
1 tablespoon finely chopped herbs such as chervil,
   parsley, chives

Preheat the oven to 200°C (400°F/Gas 6) and put a baking tray on the top shelf. Grease four ramekins with melted butter. Pour half the cream into the ramekins and then put a quarter of the mushroom, ham and cheese into each. Break an egg into each ramekin. Mix the remaining cream with the herbs and pour over the top.

Bake for 15–20 minutes on the hot baking tray, depending on how runny you like your eggs. Remove from the oven while still a little runny as the eggs will continue to cook. Season well. Serve immediately with crusty toasted bread.

SERVES 4

Croque monsieur
Pan-fried Ham and Cheese Sandwich

80 g (3 oz) unsalted butter
1 tablespoon plain (all-purpose) flour
185 ml (6 fl oz/¾ cup) milk
½ teaspoon Dijon mustard
1 egg yolk

grated nutmeg
12 slices white bread
6 slices ham
130 g (5 oz/1 cup) grated Gruyère cheese

Melt 20 g (¾ oz) of the butter in a saucepan, then add the flour and stir over low heat for 3 minutes. Slowly add the milk and Dijon mustard, whisking constantly. Leave to simmer until the mixture has thickened and reduced by about a third. Remove from the heat and stir in the egg yolk. Season with salt, pepper and the grated nutmeg and leave to cool completely.

Place half the bread slices on a baking tray. Top each piece of bread with a slice of ham, then with some of the sauce, then Gruyère and finally with another piece of bread. Melt half the remaining butter in a large frying pan and fry the sandwiches on both sides until they are golden brown, adding the remaining butter when you need it. Cut each sandwich in half to serve.

SERVES 6

Auvergne

5.00
le kilo

Roquefort
45% mg Aveyron
Réserve Mr Carlin

228.00
le k.

CHEESE

∞∞∞∞∞∞∞∞∞∞∞∞∞∞∞∞∞∞∞∞∞∞∞∞∞

France produces more than 500 types of cheeses, many of them among the world's best, and a reflection of the strength of regional traditions.

The *Appellation d'Origine Contrôlée* (AOC) is granted to quality cheeses produced in a specified region following established production methods. AOC cheeses can be distinguished by a stamp and often by wording on the package such as *Fabrication traditionnelle au lait cru avec moulé à la louche* on AOC camembert.

Fermier cheeses are farmhouse cheeses, using milk from the farmer's herd and traditional methods. Artisanal cheeses come from farmers using their own or others' milk. Coopérative cheeses are made at a dairy with the milk coming from cooperative members. Industriel cheeses are those produced in factories. Many artisanal and fermier cheesemakers have made cheeses for generations, often sold just within their region. Only a few AOC cheeses reach a wider audience. Some cheese, such as camembert, is produced by fermier, coopérative and industriel methods with very different qualities.

French cheeses are made from cow's, goat's and sheep's milk. Milk is pasteurised or lait cru (raw), which produces more complex flavours. All fermier cheeses are made of lait cru and it is compulsory for some AOC cheeses.

Cheeses are categorised into families, and looking at the rind and the texture of the pâte (inside) of a cheese can help you determine its category and therefore roughly its taste.

Fresh cheeses (fromage frais, chèvre frais) have no rind (as they haven't been ripened), and have a mild or slightly acidic taste and a high moisture content.

Pâte Fleurie (Camembert, Brie) are soft cheeses with edible white rind. These unpressed (drained naturally) cheeses are high in moisture, causing white moulds to form a rind. They have a creamy, melting pâte and sometimes a mushroom taste.

Pâte Lavée (Munster and Livarot) are soft cheeses with washed rinds. They develop a cat's-fur mould when ripening, which is washed away in a process that encourages orange bacteria to ripen the cheese from the outside in. They usually have a smooth, elastic pâte, piquant taste and pungent aroma.

Fromages de Chèvre (goat's cheeses) are unpressed cheeses that have a wrinkled rind and fresh taste when young, and a more intense, nutty, goat flavour and more wrinkled rind when older.

Pâte Persillée (Roquefort, Bleu d'Auvergne) are blue cheeses. A penicillium is introduced into the cheeses, which often spreads into blue veins. They tend to have a sharp flavour and aroma.

Pâte Pressée (Cantal, Port-du-Salut) are semi-hard cheeses with a supple rind that hardens with age. They are pressed and have a well-developed, mellow taste. The pâte varies from supple to hard.

Pâte Cuite (Beaufort, Emmental) are hard cheeses with a thick rind. These are cheeses whose curds have been finely cut, cooked and pressed. They often have a fruity or nutty flavour.

Flamiche

Cheese and Leek Pie

A speciality of the Picardie region, flamiche is made both as an open tart and a closed pie. You will usually come across it with a leek filling, as here, but it can also be made with onion or pumpkin.

1 quantity tart pastry (page 178)
500 g (1 lb 2 oz) leeks, white part only, thinly sliced
50 g (2 oz) butter
175 g (6 oz) Maroilles (soft cheese), Livarot or
    Port-Salut, chopped

1 egg
1 egg yolk
60 ml (2 fl oz/¼ cup) thick (double/heavy) cream
1 egg, lightly beaten

Preheat the oven to 180°C (350°F/Gas 4) and put a baking tray on the top shelf. Use three-quarters of the pastry to line a 23 cm (9 in) fluted loose-based tart tin.

Cook the leek in a pan of boiling salted water for 10 minutes, then drain. Heat the butter in a frying pan, add the leek and cook, stirring, for 5 minutes. Stir in the cheese. Tip into a bowl and add the egg, egg yolk and cream. Season and mix well.

Pour the filling into the pastry shell and smooth the top. Roll out the remaining pastry to cover the pie. Pinch the edges together and trim. Cut a hole in the centre and brush egg over the top. Bake for 35–40 minutes on the baking tray until browned. Leave in the tin for 5 minutes before serving.

SERVES 6

QUICHE LORRAINE
Bacon Quiche

1 quantity tart pastry (page 178)
25 g (1 oz) butter
300 g (11 oz) streaky bacon, diced

250 ml (9 fl oz/1 cup) thick (double/heavy) cream
3 eggs
grated nutmeg

Preheat the oven to 200°C (400°F/Gas 6). Line a 25 cm (10 in) fluted loose-based tart tin with the pastry. Line the pastry shell with a crumpled piece of greaseproof paper and baking beads (use dried beans or rice if you don't have beads). Blind bake the pastry for 10 minutes, then remove the paper and beads and bake for a further 3–5 minutes, or until the pastry is just cooked but still very pale. Reduce the oven to 180°C (350°F/Gas 4).

Melt the butter in a small frying pan and cook the bacon until golden. Drain on paper towels.

Mix together the cream and eggs and season with salt, pepper and nutmeg. Scatter the bacon into the pastry shell and pour in the egg mixture. Bake for 30 minutes, or until the filling is set. Leave in the tin for 5 minutes before serving.

SERVES 8

CRÊPES JAMBON-FROMAGE-CHAMPIGNON
Ham, Mushroom and Cheese Crêpes

1 quantity crêpe batter (page 178)
1 tablespoon butter
150 g (6 oz) mushrooms, sliced

2 tablespoons cream
165 g (6 oz/1 ¼ cups) grated Gruyère cheese
100 g (4 oz) ham, chopped

Heat a large crêpe or frying pan and grease with a little butter or oil. Pour in enough batter to coat the base of the pan in a thin layer and tip out any excess. Cook over moderate heat for 1 minute, or until the crêpe starts to come away from the side of the pan. Turn and cook on the other side for 1 minute, or until lightly golden. Stack the crêpes on a plate, with greaseproof paper between them, and cover with plastic wrap while you cook the rest of the batter to make six large crêpes.

Preheat the oven to 180°C (350°F/Gas 4). Heat the butter in a frying pan, add the mushrooms, season well and cook, stirring, for 5 minutes, or until the liquid has evaporated. Stir in the cream, cheese and ham.

Lay a crêpe on a board or work surface. Top with a sixth of the filling and fold into quarters. Place on a baking tray and repeat with the rest of the crêpes. Bake for 5 minutes. Serve immediately.

SERVES 6

Chapter 4

Pâtés and Terrines

*Well worth the effort involved in creating them, these dishes
are perfect picnic and buffet fare. Make them ahead of time to
allow the flavours to fully develop.*

TERRINE DE LÉGUMES SAUCE AUX FINES HERBES
Vegetable Terrine with Herb Sauce

750 g (1 lb 11 oz) carrots, cut into chunks
8 large silverbeet (Swiss chard) leaves (or 16 smaller)
12 asparagus spears
2 small zucchini (courgettes)
16 green beans, topped and tailed
250 g (9 oz) crème fraîche
6 teaspoons powdered gelatine
16 cherry tomatoes, halved

HERB SAUCE
1 tablespoon finely chopped parsley
1 tablespoon finely chopped chervil
1 tablespoon finely shredded basil
grated zest of 1 small lemon
300 g (11 oz) crème fraîche

Cook the carrot in boiling water for 25 minutes, or until tender, then drain and cool. Dip the silverbeet leaves in boiling water, then remove carefully with a slotted spoon and lay flat on paper towels.

Lightly oil a 20 x 7 x 9 cm (8 x 2¾ x 3½ in) terrine or loaf tin. Line with plastic wrap, leaving enough hanging over the sides to cover the top. Then line the tin with the silverbeet leaves, make sure there are no gaps, and leaving enough hanging over the sides to cover the top.

Trim the asparagus spears at the thicker ends so they fit the length of the terrine. Slice the zucchini in half lengthways, then into four strips. Steam the asparagus, zucchini and beans for 6 minutes, or until they are tender to the point of a knife. Drain and refresh the vegetables in cold water, then pat dry with paper towels.

Purée the carrots with the crème fraîche in a food processor, or mash and push through a sieve, and season well. Put 2 tablespoons of water in a small bowl and sprinkle with the gelatine. Leave for 5 minutes until spongy, then put the bowl over a pan of simmering water until melted. Add to the carrot purée and mix well.

Spoon one-quarter of the carrot purée into the terrine, then arrange six asparagus spears on top, all pointing in the same direction. Arrange the zucchini on top, in one flat layer. Smooth over another quarter of carrot purée, then a layer of tomatoes, cut-sides up. Spoon over another layer of carrot purée and then the beans. Arrange the rest of the asparagus spears on top and then the remaining carrot purée. Fold over the overhanging silverbeet leaves and plastic wrap to cover the top. Leave in the fridge overnight. Unmould onto a plate, peel off the plastic wrap and cut into slices.

To make the herb sauce, fold the herbs and lemon zest into the crème fraîche and season well. Serve with the vegetable terrine.

SERVES 8

Rillettes de porc
Pork Rillettes

750 g (1 lb 11 oz) pork neck or belly,
   rind and bones removed
150 g (6 oz) pork back fat
100 ml (4 fl oz) dry white wine
3 juniper berries, lightly crushed
1 teaspoon sea salt

2 teaspoons dried thyme
1/2 teaspoon ground nutmeg
1/4 teaspoon ground allspice
pinch of ground cloves
1 large garlic clove, crushed

Preheat the oven to 140°C (275°F/Gas 1). Cut the pork meat and fat into short strips and place in a casserole dish with the rest of the ingredients. Mix thoroughly. Baked, covered, for 4 hours, when the pork should be soft and surrounded by liquid fat.

Tip the meat and fat into a sieve over a bowl. Shred the meat with two forks and season if necessary.

Pack the meat into a 750 ml (27 fl oz/3 cup) dish or terrine and leave until cold. Strain the hot fat through a sieve lined with damp muslin.

Once the pork is cold, pour the fat over it (you may need to melt the fat first if it has solidified). Cover and refrigerate for up to a week. Serve at room temperature.

SERVES 8

Rillettes de canard
Duck Rillettes

600 g (1 lb 6 oz) pork belly, rind and bones removed
800 g (1 lb 13 oz) duck legs
100 ml (4 fl oz) dry white wine
1 teaspoon sea salt

1/4 teaspoon black pepper
1/2 teaspoon ground nutmeg
1/4 teaspoon ground allspice
1 large garlic clove, crushed

Preheat the oven to 140°C (275°F/Gas 1). Cut the pork into small pieces and place in a casserole dish with the rest of the ingredients and 200 ml (7 fl oz) water. Mix thoroughly. Bake, covered, for 4 hours, when the meat should be soft and surrounded by liquid fat.

Tip the meat and fat into a sieve over a bowl. Remove the meat from the duck legs and shred

all the meat with two forks. Season if necessary. Pack into a 750 ml (27 fl oz/3 cup) dish or terrine and leave until cold. Strain the hot fat through a sieve lined with damp muslin.

Once the meat is cold, pour the fat over it (you may need to melt the fat first if it has solidified). Cover and refrigerate for up to a week. Serve at room temperature.

SERVES 8

TERRINE DE CAMPAGNE
Country-style Terrine

This is the dish that you will find in restaurants if you order pâté maison. It is often served with pickled vegetables and coarse country bread. Terrine de campagne freezes very well if you have some leftover or want to make it in advance.

700 g (1 lb 9 oz) lean pork, cut into cubes
200 g (7 oz) pork belly, cut into strips
200 g (7 oz) chicken livers, trimmed
100 g (4 oz) streaky bacon, chopped
1 1/2 teaspoons sea salt
1/2 teaspoon black pepper
pinch of grated nutmeg

8 juniper berries, lightly crushed
3 tablespoons brandy
2 French shallots, finely chopped
1 large egg, lightly beaten
sprig of bay leaves
8 thinly sliced rashers streaky bacon

Put the lean pork, pork belly, chicken livers and chopped streaky bacon in a food processor and roughly chop into small dice (you will need to do this in two or three batches). Alternatively, finely dice the meat with a sharp knife.

Put the diced meat in a large bowl and add the salt, pepper, nutmeg, juniper berries and brandy. Mix carefully and leave to marinate in the fridge for at least 6 hours or overnight.

Preheat the oven to 180°C (350°F/Gas 4). Lightly butter a 20 x 7 x 9 cm (8 x 2 3/4 x 3 1/2 in) terrine or loaf tin. Add the shallots and egg to the marinated meat and carefully mix together.

Put a sprig of bay leaves in the base of the terrine and then line with the rashers of bacon, leaving enough hanging over the sides to cover the top. Spoon the filling into the terrine and then fold the bacon over the top. Cover the top with a layer of well-buttered greaseproof paper and then wrap the whole terrine in a layer of foil.

Place the terrine in a large baking dish and pour enough water into the baking dish to come halfway up the sides of the terrine. Bake for 1 1/2 hours, or until the pâté is shrinking away from the sides of the terrine.

Lift the terrine out of the bain-marie and leave the pâté to cool, wrapped in the paper and foil. Once cold, drain off the excess juices and refrigerate for up to a week. You may find that a little moisture has escaped from the pâté – this is quite normal and prevents it from drying out. Run a sharp knife around the inside of the terrine to loosen the pâté and then turn out onto a board and cut into slices.

SERVES 8

Pâté de foie de volaille
Chicken Liver Pâté

500 g (1 lb 2 oz) chicken livers
80 ml (3 fl oz/⅓ cup) brandy
90 g (3 oz) unsalted butter
1 onion, finely chopped

1 garlic clove, crushed
1 teaspoon chopped thyme
60 ml (2 fl oz/¼ cup) thick (double/heavy) cream
4 slices white bread

Trim the chicken livers, cutting away any veins and discoloured bits. Rinse, pat dry with paper towels and cut in half. Place the livers in a bowl with the brandy, cover and leave for a couple of hours. Drain the livers, reserving the brandy.

Melt half the butter in a frying pan over low heat, add the onion and garlic and cook until the onion is soft and transparent. Add the livers and thyme and stir over moderate heat until the livers change colour. Add the reserved brandy and simmer for 2 minutes. Cool for 5 minutes.

Place the livers and liquid in a food processor and whiz until smooth. Chop and add the remaining butter and process until smooth. (Alternatively, mash the livers with a fork, push through a sieve and mix with the melted butter.) Pour in the cream and process until just incorporated.

Season the pâté and spoon into an earthenware dish or terrine, smoothing the surface. Cover and refrigerate until firm. If the pâté is to be kept for more than a day, chill it and then pour clarified butter over the surface to seal.

To make Melba toasts, preheat the grill (broiler) and cut the crusts off the bread. Toast the bread on both sides and then slice horizontally with a sharp serrated knife, to give eight pieces. Carefully toast the uncooked side of each slice and then cut it into two triangles. Serve with the pâté.

SERVES 6

Far left: Gently fry the onion and garlic before adding the chicken livers and thyme.

Left: Once the livers have changed colour, add the brandy.

Terrine de saumon
Salmon Terrine

700 g (1 lb 9 oz) salmon fillet, skinned, bones removed
4 eggs
560 ml (19 fl oz/2¼ cups) thick (double/heavy) cream
10 g (½ oz) finely chopped chervil
250 g (9 oz) button mushrooms
1 teaspoon lemon juice
30 g (1 oz) butter
1 tablespoon grated onion

2 tablespoons white wine
10 large English spinach leaves
300 g (11 oz) smoked salmon, thinly sliced

LEMON MAYONNAISE
1 tablespoon lemon juice
grated zest of 1 lemon
250 ml (9 fl oz/1 cup) mayonnaise (page 182)

Preheat the oven to 170°C (325°F/Gas 3). Purée the salmon fillet and the eggs in a food processor. (Alternatively, mash with a fork.) Push the mixture through a fine sieve into a glass bowl. Place over iced water and gradually mix in the cream. Stir in the chervil, and season. Cover and chill.

Dice the mushrooms and toss with the lemon juice. Melt the butter in a frying pan and cook the onion, stirring, for 2 minutes. Add the mushrooms and cook for 4 minutes. Add the wine and cook until it has evaporated. Season and remove from the heat.

Dip the spinach leaves in boiling water, then remove with a slotted spoon and lay flat on paper towels.

Brush a 20 x 7 x 9 cm (8 x 2¾ x 3½ in) terrine or loaf tin with oil. Line the base with baking paper.

Line the base and sides with the smoked salmon, leaving enough hanging over the sides to cover the top. Half-fill the terrine with the salmon mixture. Top with half the spinach, then spread with the mushrooms and the rest of the spinach. Cover with the remaining salmon mixture, fold over the salmon and cover with buttered baking paper.

Place the terrine in a baking dish and pour water into the baking dish to come halfway up the side of the terrine. Bake for 45–50 minutes, or until a skewer inserted into the terrine comes out clean. Leave for 5 minutes before unmoulding onto a plate. Peel off the paper, cover and chill.

To make the lemon mayonnaise, stir the lemon juice and zest through the mayonnaise and serve with slices of salmon terrine.

SERVES 8

Right: Line the terrine with smoked salmon, then add a layer of salmon mixture and spinach leaves.

Far right: Once the terrine is filled, fold the smoked salmon over to cover the top.

SEAFOOD

Bordered by water on three sides, the choice of seafood available in France is rich and varied. From hearty bouillabaisse to special-occasion lobster Thermidor, there is a regional recipe for every occasion.

Coquilles Saint-Jacques Mornay
Scallops Mornay

Scallops in France are named after Saint James. Their shells were once worn by pilgrims who found them as they walked along the Spanish coast on their pilgrimage to the cathedral of Santiago de Compostela, which is dedicated to the saint.

COURT BOUILLON
250 ml (9 fl oz/1 cup) white wine
1 onion, sliced
1 carrot, sliced
1 bay leaf
4 black peppercorns

24 scallops on their shells
50 g (2 oz) butter
3 French shallots, finely chopped
3 tablespoons plain (all-purpose) flour
410 ml (14 fl oz/1²/₃ cups) milk
130 g (5 oz/1 cup) grated Gruyère cheese

To make the court bouillon, put the wine, onion, carrot, bay leaf, peppercorns and 500 ml (17 fl oz/ 2 cups) of water in a deep frying pan. Bring to the boil, then simmer for 20 minutes. Strain the court bouillon and return to the clean frying pan.

Remove the scallops from their shells. Pull away the white muscle and digestive tract from each one, leaving the roes intact. Clean the shells and keep for serving.

Bring the court bouillon to a gentle simmer over low heat, add the scallops and poach for 2 minutes. Remove the scallops from the court bouillon, then drain and return to their shells. Pour away the court bouillon.

Melt the butter in a heavy-based saucepan. Add the shallot and cook, stirring, for 3 minutes. Stir in the flour to make a roux and cook, stirring, for 3 minutes over low heat without allowing it to brown. Remove from the heat and gradually add the milk, stirring after each addition until smooth. Return to the heat and simmer, stirring, for about 3 minutes, until the sauce has thickened. Remove from the heat and stir in the cheese until melted. Season with salt and pepper.

Preheat the grill (broiler). Spoon the sauce over the scallops and place under the grill until golden brown. Serve immediately.

SERVES 6

Far left: Poach the scallops in court bouillon first, so that they are thoroughly cooked before grilling (broiling).

Left: Spoon the sauce over the scallops and grill (broil) until golden brown.

Soufflés de crabe
Crab Soufflés

1 tablespoon butter, melted
2 cloves
¼ small onion
1 bay leaf
6 black peppercorns
250 ml (9 fl oz/1 cup) milk
1 tablespoon butter

1 French shallot, finely chopped
15 g (½ oz) plain (all-purpose) flour
3 egg yolks
250 g (9 oz) cooked crab meat
pinch of cayenne pepper
5 egg whites

Preheat the oven to 200°C (400°F/Gas 6). Lightly brush six 125 ml (4 fl oz/½ cup) ramekins with the melted butter.

Press the cloves into the onion, then put in a small saucepan with the bay leaf, peppercorns and milk. Gently bring to the boil, then remove from the heat and leave to infuse for 10 minutes.

Melt the butter in a saucepan, add the shallot and cook, stirring, for 3 minutes, or until softened but not browned. Stir in the flour to make a roux and cook, stirring, for 3 minutes over low heat without allowing the roux to brown. Remove from the heat and gradually add the strained milk, stirring after each addition until smooth. Return to the heat and simmer for 3 minutes, stirring continuously. Beat in the egg yolks, one at a time, beating well after each addition.

Add the crab meat and stir until the mixture is hot and thickens (do not let it boil). Pour into a large heatproof bowl, add the cayenne and season well.

Whisk the egg whites in a clean dry bowl until they form soft peaks. Spoon a quarter of the egg white onto the crab mixture and quickly but lightly fold it in. Lightly fold in the remaining egg white. Pour into the ramekins and then run your thumb around the inside rim of each ramekin.

Put the ramekins on a baking tray and bake for 12–15 minutes, or until the soufflés are well risen and wobble slightly when tapped. Test them with a skewer inserted through a crack in the side of a soufflé – it should come out clean or slightly moist. If the skewer is still slightly moist, by the time the soufflés make it to the table they will be cooked in the centre. Serve immediately.

SERVES 6

Fold a quarter of the egg white into the soufflé mixture to loosen it up before you add the rest.

MARMITE DIEPPOISE
Normandy Fish Stew

This rich soupy stew of shellfish and fish gives away its origins in the Normandy region by its use of cider and cream. Traditionally turbot and sole are used, but the salmon adds a splash of colour.

16 mussels
12 large prawns (shrimp)
500 ml (17 fl oz/2 cups) cider or dry white wine
50 g (2 oz) butter
1 garlic clove, crushed
2 French shallots, finely chopped
2 celery stalks, finely chopped
1 large leek, white part only, thinly sliced

250 g (9 oz) small chestnut mushrooms, sliced
1 bay leaf
300 g (11 oz) salmon fillet, skinned and cut into chunks
400 g (14 oz) sole fillet, skinned and cut into thick strips
    widthways
315 ml (11 fl oz/1¼ cups) thick (double/heavy) cream
3 tablespoons finely chopped parsley

Scrub the mussels and remove their beards. Throw away any that are open and don't close when tapped on the work surface. Peel and devein the prawns.

Pour the cider or wine into a large saucepan and heat until simmering. Add the mussels, cover the pan and cook for 3–5 minutes, shaking the pan every now and then. Place a fine sieve over a bowl and pour the mussels into the sieve. Transfer the mussels to a plate, throwing away any that haven't opened in the cooking time. Strain the cooking liquid again through the sieve, leaving behind any grit or sand.

Add the butter to the cleaned pan and melt over moderate heat. Add the garlic, shallot, celery and leek and cook for 7–10 minutes, or until just soft. Add the mushrooms and cook for 4–5 minutes, until softened. While the vegetables are cooking, remove the mussels from their shells.

Add the strained liquid to the vegetables, add the bay leaf and bring to a simmer. Add the salmon, sole and prawns and cook for 3–4 minutes, or until the fish is opaque and the prawns are pink. Stir in the cream and the mussels and simmer gently for 2 minutes. Season to taste and stir in the parsley.

SERVES 6

Far left: Tip the cooked mussels into a sieve and throw away any that haven't opened.

Left: Make a sauce of the vegetables and poaching liquid, then add the seafood to cook quickly at the end.

Homard Thermidor
Lobster Thermidor

Lobster Thermidor was created for the first night celebrations of a play called 'Thermidor' in Paris in 1894. Traditionally the lobster is cut in half while alive, but freezing it first is more humane.

2 live lobsters
250 ml (9 fl oz/1 cup) fish stock
2 tablespoons white wine
2 French shallots, finely chopped
2 teaspoons chopped chervil
2 teaspoons chopped tarragon

110 g (4 oz) butter
2 tablespoons plain (all-purpose) flour
1 teaspoon dry mustard
250 ml (9 fl oz/1 cup) milk
65 g (2 oz/²/₃ cup) grated Parmesan cheese

Put the lobsters in the freezer an hour before you want to cook them. Bring a large pan of water to the boil, add the lobsters and cook for 10 minutes. Drain and cool slightly before cutting off the heads. Cut the tails in half lengthways, then use a spoon to ease the meat out of the shells and cut it into bite-sized pieces. Rinse the shells and pat dry.

Put the fish stock, white wine, shallot, chervil and tarragon into a small saucepan. Boil until reduced by half and then strain.

Melt 60 g (2 oz) of the butter in a heavy-based saucepan and stir in the flour and mustard to make a roux. Cook, stirring, for 2 minutes over low heat without allowing the roux to brown.

Remove from the heat and gradually add the milk and stock mixture, stirring after each addition until smooth. Return to the heat and stir until the sauce boils and thickens. Simmer, stirring occasionally, for 3 minutes. Stir in half the Parmesan. Season with salt and pepper.

Heat the remaining butter in a frying pan and fry the lobster over moderate heat for 2 minutes until lightly browned – take care not to overcook.

Preheat the grill (broiler). Divide half the sauce among the lobster shells, top with the lobster meat and finish with the remaining sauce. Sprinkle with the remaining Parmesan and place under the grill until golden and bubbling. Serve immediately.

SERVES 4

Right: Fry the lobster in butter until it is lightly browned, but take care not to overcook or it will toughen.

Far right: Spoon the lobster and sauce into the cleaned shells for serving.

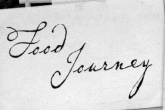

Food Journey

FROM THE SEA

∞∞∞∞∞∞∞∞∞∞∞∞∞∞∞∞∞∞∞∞∞∞∞∞∞∞∞∞∞

France is spoiled for choice when it comes to seafood, and the variety of regional fish dishes on offer along the coastline is both exciting and mouthwatering. The French certainly know how to make the best of their catch—this is a country famous for its wonderful fish dishes.

France's seafood comes from the Mediterranean to the South, the Bay of Biscay and the Atlantic Ocean to the West and the English Channel to the Northwest, as well as freshwater fish from rivers and lakes. What is not available in home waters is snapped up elsewhere, with long-distance trawlers fishing as far away as the waters of Newfoundland and Iceland.

The fishing fleets bring their catch into wholesale markets (criées), where the seafood is auctioned early in the morning and distributed to the towns and cities before daybreak. The most important of these markets is at the channel port of Boulogne, which services Paris, and also the fishing ports of Brittany and Normandy. Some of the daily catch may also be sold on the quayside, where fishermen bring their boats alongside and sell fish that are still alive from trays spilling sea water. Away from the coast, poissonneries and supermarkets sell fish and other seafood.

In the Northwest, oysters, scallops, Dublin Bay prawns, clams and whelks are found on Brittany and Normandy's plateau de fruits de mer, riches from an area that is home to some of France's most important fishing ports. Brittany fleets fish for sardines and tuna, and the area claims lobster à l'américaine as its own. Normandy is famous for its moules marinière, marmite dieppoise and its Dover sole, cooked as sole normande.

The centre of the fishing industry in the North is Boulogne, which has wonderful local sole and mussels, as well as fishing boats bringing in their catches from the Mediterranean to the Atlantic. Inland, freshwater trout, prepared 'au bleu', is a speciality of Alsace-Lorraine. In the Southwest there is Atlantic tuna from the Basque ports and oysters from Bordeaux.

Sardines and anchovies are a Southern favourite found in Languedoc-Roussillon on the Spanish border, while Provence's Mediterranean catch, from rascasse, chapon, mullet, conger eel, sea bass to bream, is transformed into wonderful dishes such as bouillabaisse and bourride.

Moules Marinière
Mussels with White Wine and Cream Sauce

2 kg (4 lb 8 oz) mussels
40 g (1 1/2 oz) butter
1 large onion, chopped
2 garlic cloves, crushed
1/2 celery stalk, chopped

410 ml (14 fl oz/1 2/3 cups) white wine
1 bay leaf
2 sprigs of thyme
185 ml (6 fl oz/3/4 cup) thick (double/heavy) cream
2 tablespoons chopped parsley

Scrub the mussels and remove the beards. Discard any that are open and don't close when tapped on the work surface.

Melt the butter in a large saucepan and cook the onion, garlic and celery, stirring occasionally, over moderate heat until the onion is softened but not browned. Add the wine, bay leaf and thyme and bring to the boil. Add the mussels, cover the pan tightly and simmer over low heat for 2–3 minutes, shaking the pan occasionally. Use tongs to lift out the mussels as they open, putting them in a warm dish. Throw away any mussels that haven't opened after 3 minutes.

Strain the liquid through a fine sieve into a clean saucepan, leaving behind any grit or sand. Bring to the boil and boil for 2 minutes. Add the cream and reheat the sauce without boiling. Season well. Serve the mussels in individual bowls with the sauce poured over. Sprinkle with the parsley and serve with plenty of bread.

SERVES 4

Sardines grillées
Grilled Sardines

8 sardines
2 tablespoons olive oil
3 tablespoons lemon juice

1/2 lemon, halved and thinly sliced
lemon wedges

Slit the sardines along their bellies and remove the guts. Rinse well and pat dry. Use scissors to cut out the gills.

Mix together the oil and lemon juice and season generously with salt and black pepper. Brush the inside and outside of each fish with the oil, then place a few lemon slices into each cavity.

Put the sardines on a preheated chargrill (griddle) and cook, basting frequently with the remaining oil, for about 2–3 minutes each side until cooked through. The sardines can also be cooked under a very hot grill (broiler). Serve with lemon wedges.

SERVES 4

Bouillabaisse

Mediterranean Fish Soup

Bouillabaisse is the most famous French fish soup and is associated with the South of the country, particularly Marseille. As a fisherman's meal it is often made with whole fish, especially rascasse (scorpion fish). Using fillets is much simpler.

ROUILLE
1 small red capsicum (pepper)
1 slice white bread, crusts removed
1 red chilli
2 garlic cloves
1 egg yolk
80 ml (3 fl oz/⅓ cup) olive oil

SOUP
18 mussels
1.5 kg (3 lb 6 oz) firm white fish fillets such as
    red mullet, bass, snapper, monkfish, rascasse,
    John Dory or eel, skin on

2 tablespoons oil
1 fennel bulb, thinly sliced
1 onion, chopped
750 g (1 lb 11 oz) ripe tomatoes
1.25 litres (44 fl oz/5 cups) fish stock or water
pinch of saffron threads
bouquet garni
5 cm (2 in) piece of orange zest

To make the rouille, preheat the grill (broiler). Cut the capsicum in half, remove the seeds and membrane and place, skin-side up, under the hot grill until the skin blackens and blisters. Leave to cool before peeling. Roughly chop the capsicum. Soak the bread in 3 tablespoons water, then squeeze dry. Put the capsicum, chilli, bread, garlic and egg yolk in a mortar and pestle or food processor and pound or mix together. Gradually add the oil in a thin stream, pounding or mixing until the rouille is smooth with the texture of thick mayonnaise. Cover and refrigerate the rouille until needed.

To make the soup, scrub the mussels and remove their beards. Discard any mussels that are already open and don't close when tapped on the work surface. Cut the fish into bite-sized pieces.

Heat the oil in a large saucepan over medium heat and cook the fennel and onion for 5 minutes, or until golden.

Score a cross in the top of each tomato. Plunge them into boiling water for 20 seconds, then drain and peel the skin away from the cross. Chop the tomatoes, discarding the cores.

Add the tomato to the pan and cook for 3 minutes. Stir in the stock, saffron, bouquet garni and orange zest, then bring to the boil and boil for 10 minutes. Discard the bouquet garni and either push the soup through a sieve or purée in a blender. Return to the clean pan, season well and bring back to the boil.

Reduce the heat to a simmer and add the fish and mussels. Cook for 5 minutes, or until the fish is tender. Throw out any mussels that haven't opened in this time. Serve the soup with rouille and bread.

SERVES 6

Chapter 6

Poultry, Meat and Game

Poultry and meat play a major role in the French diet, and there are numerous world-famous dishes that showcase them... duck à l'orange, coq au vin, boeuf bourguignon and chicken chasseur, to name a few.

Poulet à l'estragon

Tarragon Chicken

Tarragon has a delicate, but distinctive liquorice flavour and is one of the herbs found in the French fines herbes mixture. It is a particularly good partner for chicken, especially when combined with tarragon cream.

1 ½ tablespoons chopped tarragon
1 small garlic clove, crushed
50 g (2 oz) butter, softened
1 x 1.6 kg (3 lb 10 oz) chicken
2 teaspoons oil

170 ml (6 fl oz/²/₃ cup) chicken stock
2 tablespoons white wine
1 tablespoon plain (all-purpose) flour
1 tablespoon tarragon leaves
170 ml (6 fl oz/²/₃ cup) thick (double/heavy) cream

Preheat the oven to 200°C (400°F/Gas 6). Mix together the chopped tarragon, garlic and half the softened butter. Season with salt and pepper and place inside the cavity of the chicken. Tie the legs together and tuck the wing tips under.

Heat the remaining butter with the oil in a large casserole over low heat and brown the chicken on all sides. Add the chicken stock and wine. Cover the casserole and bake for 1 hour 20 minutes, or until the chicken is tender and the juices run clear when the thigh is pierced with a skewer. Remove the chicken, draining the juices into the casserole. Cover the chicken with foil and a tea towel and leave to rest.

Skim 1 tablespoon of the surface fat from the cooking liquid and put it in a small bowl. Skim the remainder of the fat from the surface and throw this away. Add the flour to the reserved fat and mix until smooth. Whisk quickly into the cooking liquid and stir over moderate heat until the sauce boils and thickens.

Strain the sauce into a clean saucepan and add the tarragon leaves. Simmer for 2 minutes, then stir in the cream and reheat without boiling. Season with salt and pepper. Carve the chicken and spoon the sauce over the top to serve.

SERVES 4

Brown the chicken to seal before adding the stock and wine.

CASSOULET

Casserole of Beans with Mixed Meats

Cassoulet takes its name from the traditional casserole dish used for cooking this stew. It varies regionally in the South of France, with the best-known versions hailing from Carcassonne, Toulouse and Castelnaudary.

400 g (14 oz/2 cups) dried haricot beans
bouquet garni
½ large onion, cut into quarters
2 garlic cloves, crushed
225 g (8 oz) salt pork or unsmoked bacon,
   cut into cubes
1 tablespoon clarified butter

400 g (14 oz) lamb shoulder
350 g (12 oz) boiling sausages (saucisses à cuire)
1 celery stalk, sliced
4 pieces duck confit (page 128) or 4 pieces roast duck
6 large tomatoes
180 g (7 oz) Toulouse sausage
4 slices baguette, made into crumbs

Put the beans in a bowl and cover with cold water. Soak overnight, then drain and rinse.

Put the drained beans in a large saucepan with the bouquet garni, onion, garlic and salt pork or bacon. Add 2–3 litres (70–105 fl oz/8–12 cups) cold water and bring to the boil, then simmer for 1 hour.

Heat the butter in a frying pan. Cut the lamb into eight pieces and brown in the butter. Add the lamb, boiling sausages, celery and duck confit to the top of the beans and push into the liquid. Score a cross in the top of each tomato, plunge them into boiling water for 20 seconds, then peel the skin away from the cross. Chop the tomatoes finely, discarding the cores, and add to the top of the cassoulet. Push into the liquid and cook for a further 1 hour.

Brown the Toulouse sausage in the frying pan and add to the top of the cassoulet. Push the sausage into the liquid and cook for 30 minutes. Preheat the oven to 160°C (315°F/Gas 2–3).

Discard the bouquet garni. Strain the liquid into a saucepan and boil over moderate heat until it is reduced by about two-thirds. Remove all the meat from the saucepan, slice the sausages and pull the duck meat from the bones. Layer all the meat and the beans, alternately, in a deep casserole. Add the liquid, to come no higher than the top of the beans.

Sprinkle the cassoulet with the breadcrumbs and bake for 40 minutes. Every 10 minutes, break the breadcrumb crust with the back of a spoon to let a little liquid through. If the beans look a bit dry, add a little stock or water to the edge of the dish. Serve straight from the casserole.

SERVES 6

BOEUF EN DAUBE

Beef Braised in Red Wine

Daubes are traditionally cooked in squat earthenware dishes called daubières, but a cast-iron casserole dish with a tight-fitting lid will work just as well. Daubes hail from Provence and are usually served with buttered macaroni or new potatoes.

MARINADE
2 cloves
1 onion, cut into quarters
500 ml (17 fl oz/2 cups) red wine
2 strips of orange zest
2 garlic cloves
1/2 celery stalk
2 bay leaves
a few parsley stalks

1.5 kg (3 lb 6 oz) beef topside, blade or rump, cut into large pieces
2 tablespoons oil
3 strips pork fat
1 pig's trotter or 225 g (8 oz) piece streaky bacon
750 ml (27 fl oz/3 cups) beef stock

To make the marinade, push the cloves into a piece of onion and mix together in a large bowl with the remaining marinade ingredients. Season the beef with salt and pepper, then add to the marinade and leave to marinate overnight.

Drain the beef and pat dry, reserving the marinade. Heat the oil in a saucepan and brown the beef in batches, then transfer it to a plate. You might need to use a little of the marinade liquid to deglaze the pan between batches to prevent the beef sticking to the bottom of the pan and burning.

Strain the marinade through a sieve into a bowl and tip the contents of the sieve into the pan to brown. Remove from the pan. Add the marinade liquid to the pan and boil, stirring, for 30 seconds to deglaze the pan.

Place the pork fat in a large casserole, along with the pig's trotter, beef and marinade solids. Add the marinade liquid and the stock. Bring to the boil, then cover, reduce the heat and simmer gently for 2–2½ hours, or until the meat is tender.

Lift the meat out of the casserole and place in a serving dish. Cover and keep warm. Remove and discard the garlic, onion, pork fat and pig's trotter. Pour the liquid through a fine sieve and skim off as much fat as possible. Return the liquid to the casserole. Bring to the boil and boil until reduced by half and syrupy. Pour the gravy over the meat to serve.

SERVES 6

Canard à l'orange
Duck à L'Orange

Duck can be fatty, which is why it should be pricked all over and cooked on a rack to let the fat drain away. The reason that duck à l'orange works so perfectly as a dish, is that the sweet acidity of the citrus fruit cuts through the rich duck fat.

5 oranges
1 x 2 kg (4 lb 8 oz) duck
2 cinnamon sticks
15 g (½ oz) mint leaves

95 g (3 oz/½ cup) light brown sugar
125 ml (4 fl oz/½ cup) cider vinegar
80 ml (3 fl oz/⅓ cup) Grand Marnier
30 g (1 oz) butter

Preheat the oven to 150°C (300°F/Gas 2). Halve two of the oranges and rub them all over the duck. Place them in the duck cavity with the cinnamon sticks and mint. Tie the legs together and tie the wings together. Prick the duck all over with a fork and place on a rack, breast-side down, in a shallow roasting tin. Roast for 45 minutes, turning the duck halfway through.

Meanwhile, zest and juice the remaining oranges (if you don't have a zester, cut the peel into strips with a sharp knife). Heat the sugar in a saucepan over low heat until it melts and caramelises: swirl the pan gently to make sure it caramelises evenly. When the sugar is a rich brown, add the vinegar (be careful as it will splutter). Boil for 3 minutes, then add the orange juice and Grand Marnier and simmer for 2 minutes.

Blanch the orange zest in a pan of boiling water for 1 minute, three times, changing the water each time. Refresh under cold water, drain and reserve.

Remove the excess fat from the tin. Increase the oven temperature to 180°C (350°F/Gas 4). Spoon some of the orange sauce over the duck and roast for 45 minutes, spooning the remaining sauce over the duck every 5–10 minutes and turning the duck to baste all sides.

Remove the duck from the oven, cover with foil and strain the juices into a saucepan. Skim off any excess fat and add the orange zest and butter to the pan. Stir to melt the butter. Reheat the sauce and serve over the duck.

SERVES 4

Add the orange juice and Grand Marnier to the sauce and simmer for 2 minutes.

Roulade de veau aux épinards et jambon

Roast Veal Stuffed with Ham and Spinach

250 g (9 oz) English spinach
100 g (4 oz) ham on the bone, diced
2 garlic cloves, crushed
2 tablespoons finely chopped parsley
2 teaspoons Dijon mustard
finely grated zest of 1 lemon
600 g (1 lb 6 oz) piece boneless veal loin or fillet, beaten
    with a meat mallet to measure 30 x 15 cm (12 x 6 in)

4 rashers streaky bacon
2 tablespoons olive oil
50 g (2 oz) butter
16 baby carrots
8 small potatoes, unpeeled
8 French shallots
185 ml (6 fl oz/¾ cup) dry (Sercial) Madeira

Preheat the oven to 170°C (325°F/Gas 3). Wash the spinach and put in a large saucepan with the water clinging to the leaves. Cover and steam for 2 minutes, until just wilted. Drain and cool, then squeeze dry. Chop and mix with the ham, garlic, parsley, mustard and lemon zest. Season well.

Spread the spinach filling over the centre of the veal. Starting from one of the shorter sides, roll up like a swiss roll. Wrap the bacon over the veal and season well. Tie with string several times to secure the bacon.

Heat the oil and half the butter in a large frying pan and add the carrots, potatoes and shallots. Briefly brown the vegetables, then tip them into a roasting tin. Brown the veal on all sides, then place on top of the vegetables. Add 4 tablespoons

of the Madeira to the pan and boil, stirring, for 30 seconds to deglaze the pan. Pour over the veal.

Roast the meat for 30 minutes, then cover it with foil to prevent overbrowning and roast for another 45–60 minutes, or until the juices run clear when you pierce the meat with a skewer in the thickest part. Wrap the meat in foil and set aside to rest. Return the vegetables to the oven if they are not yet tender.

Remove the vegetables from the roasting tin and place the tin over moderate heat. Add the rest of the Madeira and allow it to bubble, then add the remaining butter and season to taste. Slice the veal thickly and arrange on top of the vegetables. Pour over some of the Madeira sauce and serve the rest separately in a jug.

SERVES 4

Far left: Spread the spinach filling over the piece of veal and then roll up like a swiss roll.

Left: Tie with string to keep the bacon rashers in place and prevent the veal unrolling.

Poulet aux quarante gousses d'ail
Chicken with Forty Cloves of Garlic

This sounds frighteningly overpowering but, as anyone who has ever roasted garlic knows, the cloves mellow and sweeten in the oven until, when you come to serve, the creamy flesh that is squeezed from the skins is quite different from the raw clove.

2 celery stalks, including leaves
2 sprigs of rosemary
4 sprigs of thyme
4 sprigs of flat-leaf (Italian) parsley
1 x 1.6 kg (3 lb 10 oz) chicken
40 garlic cloves, unpeeled

2 tablespoons olive oil
1 carrot, roughly chopped
1 small onion, cut into 4 wedges
250 ml (9 fl oz/1 cup) white wine
1 baguette, cut into slices
small sprigs of herbs, to garnish

Preheat the oven to 200°C (400°F/Gas 6). Put a chopped celery stalk, the rosemary, half the thyme and half the parsley into the chicken cavity. Add 6 cloves of garlic. Tie the legs together and tuck the wing tips under.

Brush the chicken liberally with some of the olive oil and season well. Scatter 10 more garlic cloves over the base of a large casserole dish. Put the rest of the sprigs of herbs, chopped celery, carrot and onion in the casserole.

Put the chicken in the casserole dish on top of the herbs and vegetables. Scatter the remaining garlic cloves around the chicken and pour in the rest of the olive oil and the white wine. Cover and bake for 1 hour 20 minutes, or until the meat is tender and the juices run clear when the thigh is pierced with a skewer.

Carefully lift the chicken out of the casserole dish. Strain the juices into a small saucepan and use a pair of tongs to pick out the garlic cloves from the strained mixture. Spoon off the fat from the juices and boil for 2–3 minutes to reduce and thicken.

Cut the chicken into serving portions, pour over a little of the juices and scatter with the garlic. Toast the baguette slices, then garnish the chicken with herb sprigs and serve with the bread to be spread with the soft flesh squeezed from the garlic.

SERVES 4

Use a casserole dish into which the chicken and vegetables fit quite snugly so that the flavours mingle well.

CIVET DE CERF

Venison Casserole

This winter casserole is served up during the hunting season in popular game areas such as the Ardennes, Auvergne and Alsace. Venison benefits from being marinated before cooking, otherwise it can be a little tough.

MARINADE
½ onion
4 cloves
8 juniper berries, crushed
8 black peppercorns, crushed
250 ml (9 fl oz/1 cup) red wine
1 carrot, roughly chopped
½ celery stalk
2 bay leaves
2 garlic cloves
2 pieces lemon zest
5 sprigs of rosemary

1 kg (2 lb 4 oz) venison, cubed
30 g (1 oz) plain (all-purpose) flour
1 tablespoon oil
1 tablespoon clarified butter
8 French shallots
500 ml (17 fl oz/2 cups) brown stock
2 tablespoons redcurrant jelly
sprigs of rosemary

To make the marinade, cut the half onion into four pieces and stud each piece with a clove. Place in a large bowl and mix together with the rest of the marinade ingredients. Add the venison, toss well and leave overnight in the fridge to marinate.

Drain the venison, reserving the marinade, and pat dry with paper towels. Season the flour and use it to coat the venison.

Preheat the oven to 160°C (315°F/Gas 2–3). Heat the oil and clarified butter in a large casserole dish, brown the shallots and then remove them from the dish. Brown the venison in the oil and butter, then remove from the casserole.

Strain the marinade liquid through a sieve into the casserole and boil, stirring, for 30 seconds to deglaze. Pour in the stock and bring to the boil.

Tip the remaining marinade ingredients out of the sieve onto a piece of muslin and tie up in a parcel to make a bouquet garni. Add to the casserole with the venison. Bring the liquid to simmering point, then transfer the casserole to the oven and cook for 45 minutes. Add the shallots and cook for a further 1 hour.

Discard the bouquet garni. Remove the venison and the shallots from the cooking liquid and keep warm. Add the redcurrant jelly to the liquid and boil on the stovetop for 4–5 minutes to reduce by half. Strain the sauce and pour over the venison. Serve garnished with sprigs of rosemary.

SERVES 4

Carbonnade de Boeuf

Beef Carbonnade

This is a Flemish recipe, but it is also traditional throughout the North of France. Carbonnade means 'charcoal cooked' but this is, in fact, a rich oven-cooked stew of beef in beer. Delicious with jacket potatoes.

30 g (1 oz) butter
2–3 tablespoons oil
1 kg (2 lb 4 oz) lean beef rump or chuck steak, cubed
4 onions, chopped
1 garlic clove, crushed
1 teaspoon brown sugar
1 tablespoon plain (all-purpose) flour

500 ml (17 fl oz/2 cups) beer (bitter or stout)
2 bay leaves
4 sprigs of thyme

CROUTONS
6–8 slices baguette
Dijon mustard

Preheat the oven to 150°C (300°F/Gas 2). Melt the butter in a large sauté pan over high heat with 1 tablespoon of the oil. Brown the meat in batches and then lift out onto a plate.

Add another tablespoon of oil to the pan and add the onion. Cook over moderate heat for 10 minutes, then add the garlic and sugar and cook for another 5 minutes, adding another tablespoon of oil if it is needed. Lift out the onion onto a second plate.

Reduce the heat to low and pour in any juices that have drained from the browned meat, then stir in the flour. Remove from the heat and stir in the beer, a little at a time (the beer will foam). Return

to the heat and let the mixture gently simmer and thicken. Season with salt and pepper.

Layer the meat and onion in a casserole dish, tucking the bay leaves and thyme sprigs between the layers and seasoning with salt and pepper as you go. Pour the liquid over the meat, cover and bake for 2½–3 hours, or until the meat is tender.

To make the croutons, preheat the grill (broiler). Lightly toast the baguette on both sides, then spread one side with mustard. Arrange on top of the carbonnade, mustard-side up, and place the casserole under the grill for 1 minute.

SERVES 4

Layer the meat and onion in the dish, adding the herbs and seasoning between the layers.

SON DE HAUTE-LOIR
ATION TRADITIONN
Saucissons
50
EXPRESS
Sergio
Tacchini
-Ane
-Chevreuil
-Sangier
Saucisson au Herbes
30F,00 Pièce
50F,00 les 2
Saucisson au Noix
30,00 Pièce
Saucisson au Comté
50,00 les 2
=

Food Journey

CHARCUTERIE

ﾟ°ｏ°ｏ°ｏ°ｏ°ｏ°ｏ°ｏ°ｏ°ｏ°ｏ°ｏ°ｏ°ｏ°ｏ°ｏ°ｏ°ｏ°ｏ°ｏ

In France, almost every village has a charcuterie selling fresh and air-dried sausages, hams and pâtés, and the art of the artisan charcutier lives on in a wealth of special local and regional charcuterie.

Meaning literally 'cured meat', charcuterie refers to cured or cooked pork products, though other meats can be used, from game and beef in sausages, to goose and duck in foie gras and pâtés. Traditionally horse and donkey meat were also used, but this is now rare. Charcuterie is associated with pork more than any other meat as virtually any part of a pig can be transformed into someting to eat. Pigs have traditionally been kept by rural families and slaughtered in autumn, the fresh meat eaten and the rest made into items that could be preseved and eaten through winter.

Charcuterie is made commercially as well as by artisan charcutiers all over France. In the Northeast, charcuterie from Alsace is influenced by Germanic traditions, while the forests of the Ardennes have provided game, such as wild boar, for hams and pâtés. The Northwest is famous for rillettes from Tours and Vouvray, and the Southwest for its duck and goose foie gras and Bayonne ham. The East, specifically Lyon, is the acknowledged home of charcuterie, and its andouillettes, Jésus, cervelas and rosettes are well known all over France. The South makes saucissons secs and air-dried hams.

Saucisses, or fresh sausages, vary from the coarse pork saucisse de Toulouse to the frankfurter-like saucisse de Strasbourg. Boudin noir, a kind of black pudding, and boudin blanc are sausage-like charcuterie; andouilles and andouillettes are made from chitterlings or tripe. Fresh sausages are often poached rather than grilled (broiled) and these saucisses à cuire (boiling sausages) are generally larger and fatty and used in dishes such as potato salad, choucroute garnie or cassoulet.

Saucissons secs, or dried sausages, are like Italian salamis and are usually cured by air-drying. They need no cooking and are sliced and eaten cold. Most are made from pork, though some include horse meat or beef. Spicing and flavouring varies regionally. Lyon is a centre for this charcuterie, including rosettes and Jésus, and elsewhere other products include pork and beef saucisson d'Arles from Provence; French and German-influenced saucissons from Alsace; and rustic, coarse sausages from Limousin and the Auvergne.

Hams have been made in France since before the Romans. Jambon de Bayonne is probably the best-known jambon cru (raw ham), air-dried and sweet like Parma ham. Alsace and the Ardennes are famous for jambon cru fumé (smoked raw hams).

Originally meaning more a 'pie' (now called pâté en croûte), pâté now refers only to the filling and is similar to a terrine.

Fattened duck and goose livers, a speciality of Southwest France, are sold on their own or made into parfait or pâté. Confit is made from pork, duck or goose meat cooked in its own fat and used in cassoulet and garbure, a hearty cabbage soup.

Magrets de canard aux cassis et aux framboises

Duck Breasts with Cassis and Raspberries

Magret is the French name for duck breast, the leanest part of the duck. Magret de canard is usually served pink with a well-crisped skin. You can use frozen raspberries for this recipe, but make sure they are thoroughly defrosted.

4 x 200 g (7 oz) duck breasts
2 teaspoons sea salt
2 teaspoons ground cinnamon
1 tablespoon demerara sugar

250 ml (9 fl oz/1 cup) red wine
170 ml (6 fl oz/²/₃ cup) crème de cassis
1 tablespoon cornflour (cornstarch) or arrowroot
250 g (9 oz) raspberries

Score the duck breasts through the skin and fat, without cutting all the way through to the meat. Heat a frying pan and fry the duck breasts, skin-side down, until the skin browns and the fat runs out. Lift the duck out of the pan and tip away most of the fat.

Combine the sea salt, cinnamon and demerara sugar. Sprinkle over the skin of the duck breasts, then press in with your hands. Season with black pepper. Reheat the frying pan and cook the duck breasts, skin-side up, for 10–15 minutes. Lift out of the frying pan and leave to rest on a carving board. Preheat the grill (broiler).

Meanwhile, combine the red wine and cassis in a jug. Pour about 80 ml (3 fl oz/¹/₃ cup) of the liquid

into a small bowl and mix in the cornflour or arrowroot, then pour this back into the jug.

Pour the excess fat out of the frying pan to leave about 2 tablespoons. Return the pan to the heat and pour in the red wine and cassis. Simmer for 2–3 minutes, stirring constantly, until the sauce has thickened. Add the raspberries and simmer for another minute, to warm the fruit through. Check the seasoning.

Grill (broil) the duck breasts, skin-side up, for 1 minute, or until the sugar starts to caramelise. Slice the duck breasts thinly, pour a little sauce over the top and serve the rest in a jug.

SERVES 4

Poulet vallée d'Auge

Chicken with Calvados

This is one of the classic dishes of Normandy and Brittany, the famous apple-growing regions of France. If you hear it referred to as poulet au cidre, this means the chicken has been cooked in cider rather than stock.

1 x 1.6 kg (3 lb 10 oz) chicken
2 dessert apples
1 tablespoon lemon juice
60 g (2 oz) butter
½ onion, finely chopped

½ celery stalk, finely chopped
1 tablespoon plain (all-purpose) flour
80 ml (3 fl oz/⅓ cup) Calvados or brandy
375 ml (13 fl oz/1½ cups) chicken stock
80 ml (3 fl oz/⅓ cup) crème fraîche

Joint the chicken into eight pieces by removing the legs and cutting between the drumstick and thigh joint. Cut down either side of the backbone and lift it out. Turn the chicken over and cut through the cartilage down the centre of the breastbone. Cut each breast in half, leaving the wing attached.

Peel and core the apples. Finely chop half of one apple. Cut the rest into 12 wedges. Toss the apple in the lemon juice.

Heat half the butter in a large frying pan and cook the chicken, skin-side down, until golden. Turn and cook for 5 minutes. Remove the chicken and pour off the fat. Heat 1 tablespoon butter in the same pan and fry the onion, celery and chopped apple for 5 minutes without browning.

Remove from the heat and stir in the flour. Add the Calvados and return to the heat. Gradually stir in the chicken stock. Bring to the boil, return the chicken to the pan, cover and simmer gently for 15 minutes, or until tender and cooked through.

Meanwhile, heat the remaining butter in a small frying pan. Add the apple wedges and fry them over moderate heat until browned and tender. Remove from the pan and keep warm.

Remove the chicken from the pan and keep warm. Skim the excess fat from the cooking liquid in the pan. Add the crème fraîche, bring to the boil and boil for 4 minutes, or until thick enough to lightly coat the back of a wooden spoon. Season and pour over the chicken. Serve with the apple wedges.

SERVES 4

Right: Add the chicken pieces and cook until golden.

Far right: Sprinkle the flour over the fried onion, celery and chopped apple and stir to combine.

CHOUCROUTE GARNIE

Sauerkraut with Mixed Pork Products

Sauerkraut (choucroute), or pickled cabbage, is an important ingredient in Alsace cuisine. This dish can vary according to the number of people you want to feed. Traditionally, the more people there are, the wider the variety of meat used.

1.25 kg (2 lb 13 oz) fresh or tinned sauerkraut
4 tablespoons bacon fat or lard
1 onion, chopped
1 large garlic clove, crushed
1 onion, studded with 4 cloves
1 ham knuckle or hock
2 bay leaves
2 carrots, diced

8 juniper berries, lightly crushed
1 x 450 g (1 lb) piece pork shoulder
450 g (1 lb) salt pork belly, cut into thick strips
185 ml (6 fl oz/³/₄ cup) dry wine, preferably Riesling
12 small potatoes, unpeeled
3 boiling sausages (saucisses à cuire)
6 frankfurters

If using fresh sauerkraut, wash it under cold water, then squeeze dry. If using a tin or jar of sauerkraut, simply drain it well.

Preheat the oven to 190°C (375°F/Gas 5). Melt the fat or lard in a large casserole, add the chopped onion and garlic and cook for 10 minutes, or until soft but not browned. Remove and set aside half the onion. Add half the sauerkraut to the casserole, then place the whole onion and ham knuckle on top. Scatter with the bay leaves, carrot and juniper berries. Season. Add the rest of the onion and the remaining sauerkraut and season again. Place the pork shoulder and strips of pork belly on top.

Pour in the wine and 125 ml (4 fl oz/¹/₂ cup) water. Bake, covered, for 2¹/₂ hours (add more water after 1 hour if necessary). Add the potatoes and cook for 30–40 minutes, or until the potatoes are tender.

Poach the boiling sausages in simmering water for 20 minutes, then add the frankfurters and poach for a further 10 minutes. Drain and keep warm. Discard the studded onion from the casserole.

Cut any meat from the ham knuckle or hock and slice the pork shoulder and the sausages. Arrange the piping hot sauerkraut on a large dish with the potatoes, sausages and pieces of meat.

SERVES 8

Place the ham knuckle on top of the sauerkraut and add the other flavourings, then layer with the rest of the onion, sauerkraut and pork shoulder and belly.

Noisettes de porc aux pruneaux

Pork Noisettes with Prunes

Pork with prunes is a typical dish of the orchard-rich Touraine region. It is sometimes said that the French generally do not combine fruit with meat, sweet flavours with savoury, but prunes and apples are both enthusiastically combined with pork.

8 pork noisettes or 2 x 400 g (14 oz) pork fillets
16 prunes, pitted
1 tablespoon oil
50 g (2 oz) butter
1 onion, finely chopped

150 ml (6 fl oz) white wine
280 ml (10 fl oz) chicken or brown stock
1 bay leaf
2 sprigs of thyme
250 ml (9 fl oz/1 cup) thick (double/heavy) cream

Trim all the excess fat from the pork, making sure that you get rid of any membrane that will cause the pork to shrink. If you are using pork fillet, cut each fillet into four diagonal slices. Put the prunes in a small saucepan, cover with cold water and then bring to the boil. Reduce the heat and simmer the prunes for 5 minutes. Drain well.

Heat the oil in a large heavy-based frying pan and add half the butter. When the butter starts to foam, sauté the pork, in batches if necessary, on both sides until cooked. Transfer to a warm plate, cover and keep warm.

Pour the excess fat from the pan. Melt the rest of the butter, add the onion and cook over low heat until softened but not browned. Add the wine and bring to the boil, then simmer for 2 minutes. Add the stock, bay leaf and thyme and bring to the boil. Reduce the heat and simmer for 10 minutes, or until reduced by half.

Strain the stock into a bowl. Return the stock to the cleaned pan, add the cream and prunes and simmer for 8 minutes, or until the sauce thickens slightly. Return the pork to the pan and simmer until heated through.

SERVES 4

Right: Sauté the pork on both sides, then keep it warm while you make the sauce.

Far right: Add the stock, bay leaf and thyme to the sauce and simmer until reduced by half.

Navarin à la Printanière

Lamb Stew with Spring Vegetables

Navarin à la printanière is traditionally made to welcome spring and the new crop of young vegetables. Navarins, or stews, can also be made all year round, using older winter root vegetables such as potatoes, carrots and turnips.

1 kg (2 lb 4 oz) lean lamb shoulder
30 g (1 oz) butter
1 onion, chopped
1 garlic clove, crushed
1 tablespoon plain (all-purpose) flour
500 ml (17 fl oz/2 cups) brown stock

bouquet garni
18 baby carrots
8 large-bulb spring onions
200 g (7 oz) baby turnips
175 g (6 oz) small potatoes
150 g (6 oz) peas, fresh or frozen

Trim the lamb of any fat and sinew and then cut it into bite-sized pieces. Heat the butter over high heat in a large casserole. Brown the lamb in two or three batches, then remove from the casserole.

Add the onion to the casserole and cook, stirring occasionally, over moderate heat for 3 minutes, or until softened but not browned. Add the garlic and cook for a further minute, or until aromatic.

Return the meat and juices to the casserole and sprinkle with the flour. Stir over high heat until the meat is well coated and the liquid is bubbling, then gradually stir in the stock. Add the bouquet garni and bring to the boil. Reduce the heat to low, cover the casserole and cook for 1¼ hours.

Trim the carrots, leaving a little bit of green stalk, and do the same with the spring onions and baby turnips. Cut the potatoes in half if they are large.

Add the vegetables to the casserole, bring to the boil and simmer, covered, for 15 minutes, or until the vegetables are tender. (If you are using frozen peas, add them right at the end so they just heat through.) Season with plenty of salt and pepper before serving.

SERVES 6

Far left: Brown the lamb in a couple of batches so that you don't lower the temperature by overcrowding.

Left: Once the meat is browned and coated with flour, slowly stir in the stock.

BLANQUETTE DE VEAU

Creamy Veal Stew

Blanquettes are usually served with plain white rice or boiled new potatoes. They can vary from region to region, but this one with mushrooms and onions and a sauce thickened with cream and eggs is a classic recipe.

800 g (1 lb 13 oz) boneless veal shoulder,
   cut into 3 cm (1¼ in) cubes
1 litre (35 fl oz/4 cups) brown stock
4 cloves
½ large onion
1 small carrot, roughly chopped
1 leek, white part only, roughly chopped
1 celery stalk, roughly chopped
1 bay leaf
30 g (1 oz) butter
30 g (1 oz/¼ cup) plain (all-purpose) flour
1 tablespoon lemon juice

1 egg yolk
2½ tablespoons thick (double/heavy) cream

ONION GARNISH
250 g (9 oz) pickling or pearl onions
10 g (½ oz) butter
1 teaspoon caster (superfine) sugar

MUSHROOM GARNISH
10 g (½ oz) butter
2 teaspoons lemon juice
150 g (6 oz) button mushrooms, trimmed

Put the veal in a large saucepan, cover with water and bring to the boil. Drain, rinse well and drain again. Return to the pan and add the stock. Press the cloves into the onion and add to the pan with the remaining vegetables and bay leaf.

Bring to the boil, then reduce the heat, cover and simmer the veal for 40–60 minutes, or until it is tender. Skim the surface occasionally. Strain the veal, reserving the cooking liquid and throwing away the vegetables. Keep the veal warm.

To make the onion garnish, put the onions in a small pan with enough water to half cover them. Add the butter and sugar. Place a crumpled piece of greaseproof paper directly over the top of the onions. Bring to a simmer and cook over low heat for 20 minutes, or until the water has evaporated and the onions are tender.

To make the mushroom garnish, half-fill a small pan with water and bring it to the boil. Add the butter, lemon juice and mushrooms and simmer for 3 minutes, or until the mushrooms are tender. Drain the mushrooms, discarding the liquid.

Heat the butter in a large pan. Stir in the flour to make a roux and then cook, stirring, for 3 minutes without allowing the roux to brown. Remove from the heat and gradually add the reserved cooking liquid, stirring after each addition until smooth. Return to the heat and whisk until the sauce comes to the boil. Reduce the heat to low and simmer for 8 minutes, or until it coats the back of the spoon.

Add the lemon juice and season well. Quickly stir in the egg yolk and cream, then add the veal and the onion and mushroom garnishes. Reheat gently, without boiling, to serve.

SERVES 6

ROGNONS D'AGNEAU TURBIGO

Kidneys Turbigo

This stew of kidneys, sausages and onions is named after the town of Turbigo in Lombardy, the site of two famous French military victories over the Austrian army in the nineteenth century.

8 lamb's kidneys
60 g (2 oz) butter
8 chipolata sausages
12 small pickling or pearl onions or French shallots
125 g (5 oz) button mushrooms, sliced
1 tablespoon plain (all-purpose) flour
2 tablespoons dry sherry
2 teaspoons tomato paste (concentrated purée)

250 ml (9 fl oz/1 cup) beef stock
2 tablespoons finely chopped parsley

CROUTES
oil, for brushing
2 garlic cloves, crushed
12 slices baguette, cut on an angle

Trim, halve and cut the white membrane from the kidneys with scissors. Heat half of the butter in a large frying pan. Cook the kidneys for 2 minutes, or until browned all over. Remove to a plate. Add the chipolatas to the pan and cook for 2 minutes, or until browned all over. Remove to a plate. Cut in half on the diagonal.

Lower the heat and add the remaining butter to the pan. Cook the onions and mushrooms, stirring, for 5 minutes, or until soft and golden brown.

Mix together the flour and sherry to make a paste. Add the tomato paste and stock. Mix until smooth.

Remove the pan from the heat. Stir in the stock mixture, return to the heat and stir until boiling and slightly thickened. Season well. Return the kidneys and chipolatas to the frying pan. Lower the heat, cover and simmer, stirring occasionally for 25 minutes, or until the kidneys are cooked.

Meanwhile, to make the croutes, preheat the oven to 180°C (350°F/Gas 4). Mix together the oil and garlic and brush over the bread slices. Place on a baking tray and bake for 3–4 minutes. Turn over and bake for a further 3 minutes, or until golden brown. Sprinkle the kidneys with parsley and serve with the croutes on one side.

SERVES 4

Far left: Cook the halved kidneys in the butter until they are browned all over.

Left: Cook the onions and mushrooms in more of the butter until they are soft and golden brown.

Fricassée de lapin

Rabbit Fricassée

The name of the dish comes from an old French word, fricasser, to fry. A fricassée is a dish of white meat, usually chicken, veal or rabbit, in a velouté sauce with egg yolks and cream. Wild rabbit, if you can get it, has a better flavour than farmed.

60 g (2 oz) clarified butter
1 x 1.5 kg (3 lb 6 oz) rabbit, cut into 8 pieces
200 g (7 oz) button mushrooms
80 ml (3 fl oz/¹⁄₃ cup) white wine
170 ml (6 fl oz/²⁄₃ cup) chicken stock

bouquet garni
80 ml (3 fl oz/¹⁄₃ cup) oil
a small bunch of sage
125 ml (4 fl oz/¹⁄₂ cup) thick (double/heavy) cream
2 egg yolks

Heat half the clarified butter in a large saucepan. Season the rabbit and brown in batches, turning once. Remove from the saucepan and set aside. Add the remaining butter to the pan and brown the mushrooms.

Put the rabbit back into the saucepan with the mushrooms. Add the wine and boil for a couple of minutes before adding the stock and bouquet garni. Cover the pan tightly and simmer gently over very low heat for 40 minutes.

Meanwhile, heat the oil in a small saucepan. Remove the leaves from the bunch of sage and drop them, a few at a time, into the hot oil. The leaves will immediately start to bubble around the edges. Cook them for 30 seconds, or until

bright green and crisp. Don't overheat the oil or cook the leaves for too long or they will turn black and taste burnt. Drain on paper towels and then sprinkle with salt.

Remove the cooked rabbit and mushrooms from the pan and keep warm. Discard the bouquet garni. Remove the pan from the heat. Mix together the cream and egg yolks and stir quickly into the stock. Return the pan to very low heat and cook, stirring, for about 5 minutes to thicken slightly (don't let the sauce boil or the eggs will scramble). Season with salt and pepper.

To serve, pour the sauce over the rabbit and mushrooms and garnish with the sage leaves.

SERVES 4

Right: Add the stock and bouquet garni to the rabbit before simmering gently.

Far right: While the rabbit is simmering, deep-fry the sage leaves until crisp.

WINE

France is indisputably the centre of the wine world, and great Bordeaux, Burgundies and Champagnes continue to set the standards all others aspire to.

The French were making wines from indigenous vines before even the Romans arrived. Over the centuries, wine-makers have cultivated an incredible number of grape varieties, eventually matching each one to the right methods of production, the perfect climate and terrain, from the wet North to the cool mountains and the hot Mediterranean. This means that today France produces nearly every classic wine in the world.

The French *Appellation d'Origine Contrôlée* (AOC) is the oldest and most precise wine-governing body in the world. The French attach much importance to the notion of 'terroir', the belief that there is a perfect environment in which to grow a wine and that every wine should demonstrate the character of that environment. Thus, the smaller and more pinpointed an appellation is, the more prestigious it is considered to be. Within the Bordeaux AOC, sub-regions, such as Médoc, and even individual communities within this, such as Pauillac, may gain their own appellation. The AOC also defines grape varieties, yields and production methods.

Vin Délimité de Qualité Supérieure (VDQS) classifies the less distinguished regions standing between AOC and *vins de pays* status. *Vins de pays* (country wines) can be great if they have a strong local character. *Vins de table* should be drinkable.

READING FRENCH LABELS

Château: a Bordeaux wine estate

Clos: on some Burgundies, meaning a walled vineyard

Cru: meaning 'growth', it refers to wine from a single estate

Cru Bourgeois: an unofficial level of classification just below Bordeaux's crus classés

Grand Cru Classé/Cru Classé: a Bordeaux classified in 1855, usually of a very high quality. Also used in other regions to signify their most prestigious wines

Cuvée: a blended wine from different grapes or vineyards

Cuvée Prestige: a special vintage or blend

Millésimé: vintage

Mis en Bouteille au Château/Domaine: estate-bottled, rather than a merchant or cooperative blend

Négociant-Éleveur: a wine merchant, often an international firm, who buys grapes to blend and age and then produces their own wine.

Propriétaire-Récoltant: growers who make their own wine

BOEUF BOURGUIGNON

Beef Stewed in Red Wine

Almost every region of France has its own style of beef stew, but Burgundy's version is the most famous. If you can, make it a day in advance to let the flavours develop. Serve with a salad of endive, chicory and watercress and bread or new potatoes.

1.5 kg (3 lb 6 oz) beef blade or chuck steak
750 ml (27 fl oz/3 cups) red wine (preferably Burgundy)
3 garlic cloves, crushed
bouquet garni
70 g (2 oz) butter
1 onion, chopped

1 carrot, chopped
2 tablespoons plain (all-purpose) flour
200 g (7 oz) bacon, cut into short strips
300 g (11 oz) French shallots, peeled but left whole
200 g (7 oz) small button mushrooms

Cut the steak into 4 cm (1½ in) cubes and trim away any excess fat. Put the meat, wine, garlic and bouquet garni in a large bowl, cover with plastic wrap and leave in the fridge for at least 3 hours, preferably overnight.

Preheat the oven to 160°C (315°F/Gas 2–3). Drain the meat, reserving the marinade and bouquet garni. Dry the meat on paper towels. Heat 30 g (1 oz) of the butter in a large casserole dish. Add the onion, carrot and bouquet garni and cook over low heat, stirring occasionally, for 10 minutes. Remove from the heat.

Heat 20 g (1 oz) of the butter in a large frying pan over high heat. Fry the meat in batches for about 5 minutes, or until well browned. Add all the meat to the casserole dish.

Pour the reserved marinade into the frying pan and boil, stirring, for 30 seconds to deglaze the pan. Remove from the heat. Return the casserole to high heat and sprinkle the meat and vegetables with the flour. Cook, stirring constantly, until the meat is well coated with the flour. Pour in the marinade and stir well. Bring to the boil, stirring constantly, then cover and cook in the oven for 2 hours.

Heat the remaining butter in the cleaned frying pan and cook the bacon and shallots, stirring, for 8–10 minutes, or until the shallots are softened but not browned. Add the mushrooms to the pan and cook, stirring occasionally, for 2–3 minutes, or until browned. Drain the mixture on paper towels, then add to the casserole.

Cover the casserole and return to the oven for 30 minutes, or until the meat is soft and tender. Discard the bouquet garni. Season and skim any fat from the surface before serving.

SERVES 6

Confit de Canard

Duck Confit

A confit is the traditional method of preserving meat for use throughout the year. Today it is still a delicious way to cook and eat duck. The thighs and legs are usually preserved, with the breast being served fresh.

8 large duck legs
8 tablespoons coarse sea salt
12 bay leaves

8 sprigs of thyme
16 juniper berries, lightly crushed
2 kg (4 lb 8 oz) duck or goose fat, cut into pieces

Put the duck legs in a bowl or dish in which they fit snuggly. Scatter the salt over the top and season with black pepper. Tuck half the bay leaves, thyme sprigs and juniper berries into the dish. Cover and leave in the fridge overnight.

Preheat the oven to 180°C (350°F/Gas 4). Put the duck legs into a large roasting tin, leaving behind the herbs and any liquid in the bowl. Add the duck or goose fat to the tin and roast for 1 hour. Reduce the oven to 150°C (300°F/Gas 2) and then roast the duck for a further 2 hours, basting occasionally, until the duck is very well cooked.

Wash one large (or two smaller) kilner jars and dry in the hot oven for 5 minutes to sterilise them.

Use tongs to put the hot duck legs in the hot jar. Add the remaining bay leaves, thyme sprigs and juniper berries. Strain the cooking fat through a sieve and into a large jug. Now pour the fat into the jar to cover the duck. Close the lid and leave to cool. The fat will solidify on cooling.

The duck confit will keep for several months in a cool pantry or fridge. To use, remove as much of the duck as you need from the jar, returning any excess fat to cover the remaining duck. The meat can then be roasted in a very hot oven until really crisp and served with lentils, beans or salad. Or the duck can be used to make cassoulet.

SERVES 8

Right: Roast the duck legs until they are very well cooked.

Far right: Use tongs to push the duck legs into the jars and cover with the strained hot fat to seal.

GIGOT D'AGNEAU PRINTANIER

Roast Leg of Lamb with Spring Vegetables

A popular meat in France, lamb comes in various guises. In some areas it feeds on lush grasslands and, in others, on wild herbs. In Normandy, Picardie and Bordeaux, pré-salé lambs feed on salt marshes and are often served without added flavourings.

1 x 2 kg (4 lb 8 oz) leg of lamb
3 sprigs of rosemary
6 garlic cloves, unpeeled
500 g (1 lb 2 oz) small potatoes, halved
250 g (9 oz) baby carrots

6 small leeks
250 g (9 oz) small zucchini (courgettes)
1 ½ tablespoons plain (all-purpose) flour
125 ml (4 fl oz/½ cup) red wine
170 ml (6 fl oz/²/₃ cup) brown stock

Preheat the oven to 200°C (400°F/Gas 6). Rub the lamb all over with salt and pepper. Put the lamb in a roasting tin, lay the sprigs of rosemary on top and scatter the garlic around the lamb. Roast for 20 minutes, then turn the lamb over.

Add the potatoes to the roasting tin and toss in the lamb fat, then return to the oven for another 15 minutes. Turn the lamb again and cook for a further 15 minutes.

Add the baby carrots and leeks to the tin, toss with the potatoes in the lamb fat and turn the lamb again. Roast for 15 more minutes, then add the zucchini. Toss all the vegetables in the lamb fat and turn the leg of lamb again.

Roast for another 15 minutes, then lift the lamb out of the tin to rest. The lamb will be rare – if you prefer, cook it for another 5–10 minutes. Remove the vegetables and garlic from the roasting tin and keep warm.

To make the gravy, spoon the fat from the surface of the meat juices. Place the roasting tin on the stovetop over moderate heat and stir in the flour to make a roux. Cook, stirring, for 2 minutes and then gradually stir in the wine and stock. Boil the gravy for 2 minutes, then strain into a serving jug.

Carve the lamb and serve with the vegetables and garlic. Serve the gravy separately.

SERVES 6

Far left: Season the lamb generously and roast with just the rosemary and garlic for 20 minutes.

Left: Add the vegetables in stages, depending on how long they take to cook.

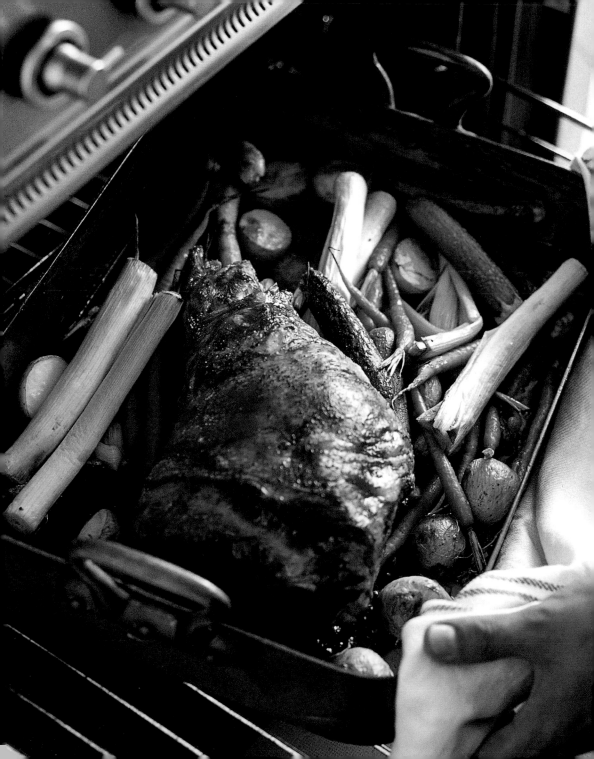

Poulet sauce chasseur

Chicken Chasseur

Chasseur means 'hunter' and is a term used for dishes including mushrooms, shallots, tomatoes, wine and brandy. The name is likely to be a reference to the fact that this was originally a recipe for cooking game.

1 x 1.6 kg (3 lb 10 oz) chicken
1 tablespoon oil
60 g (2 oz) butter
2 French shallots, finely chopped
125 g (5 oz) button mushrooms, sliced
1 tablespoon plain (all-purpose) flour
125 ml (4 fl oz/½ cup) white wine
2 tablespoons brandy

2 teaspoons tomato paste (concentrated purée)
250 ml (9 fl oz/1 cup) chicken stock
2 teaspoons chopped tarragon
1 teaspoon chopped parsley

CROUTONS
2 slices bread
olive oil

Joint the chicken into eight pieces by removing both the legs and cutting between the joint of the drumstick and the thigh. Cut down either side of the backbone and lift it out. Turn the chicken over and cut through the cartilage down the centre of the breastbone. Cut each chicken breast in half, leaving the wing attached to the top half.

Heat the oil in a frying pan or saucepan and add half the butter. Once the foaming has subsided, add the chicken pieces and sauté in batches until browned all over. Transfer all of the chicken to a plate and keep warm. Pour the excess fat out of the pan.

Melt the remaining butter in the pan, add the shallots and cook gently until they are softened but not browned. Add the mushrooms and cook, covered, over moderate heat for 3 minutes.

Add the flour and cook, stirring constantly, for 1 minute. Stir in the wine, brandy, tomato paste and stock. Bring to the boil, stirring constantly, reduce the heat, add the tarragon and season.

Return the chicken to the pan, cover and simmer for 30 minutes, or until the chicken is tender and cooked through. Sprinkle with parsley to serve.

To make the croutons, trim the crusts from the bread and cut the bread into moon shapes with a biscuit cutter. Heat the olive oil in a frying pan and fry the bread until golden. Drain on paper towels and serve hot with the chicken.

SERVES 4

Petit salé aux lentilles
Salt Pork with Lentils

It is thought that the dry climate and volcanic soil around the town of Le Puy-en-Velay in the Auvergne are the favourable conditions that allow the region's superior green lentil to grow. They are a more expensive variety, but have a superb flavour.

1 kg (2 lb 4 oz) salt pork belly, cut into thick strips
1 small salt pork knuckle
1 large carrot, cut into chunks
200 g (7 oz) swede (rutabaga) or turnips, peeled and cut into chunks
100 g (4 oz) leek, white part only, thickly sliced
1 parsnip, cut into chunks

1 onion, studded with 4 cloves
1 garlic clove
bouquet garni
2 bay leaves
6 juniper berries, slightly crushed
350 g (12 oz) puy lentils
2 tablespoons chopped parsley

Depending on the saltiness of the pork you are using, you may need to soak it in cold water for several hours or blanch it before using. Ask your butcher whether to do this.

Put the pork in a large saucepan along with the vegetables, bouquet garni, bay leaves and juniper berries. Stir thoroughly, then add enough water to cover the ingredients. Bring to the boil, then reduce the heat, cover and simmer gently for 1¼ hours.

Put the lentils in a sieve and rinse with cold water. Add to the saucepan and stir, then replace the lid and simmer for a further 45–50 minutes, or until the pork and lentils are tender.

Drain the mixture into a colander, discarding all of the liquid. Return the contents of the colander to the saucepan. Discard the whole onion. Season the pork and lentils with plenty of black pepper and taste to see if it needs salt. Stir in the parsley.

SERVES 6

Right: Use a saucepan that is large enough to fit all of the ingredients comfortably.

Far right: Unlike other varieties, puy lentils keep their shape when cooked.

BOEUF EN CROÛTE

Beef Fillet in Pastry

For this dish to work really well, you need to ask the butcher for a piece of centre-cut beef fillet that is an even thickness all the way along. The pastry can be puff, flaky or even brioche dough. Beef Wellington is the English equivalent.

PÂTÉ
180 g (7 oz) butter
3 French shallots, chopped
1 garlic clove, chopped
360 g (12 oz) chicken livers
1 tablespoon brandy or Cognac

1 x 1 kg (2 lb 4 oz) thick beef fillet
30 g (1 oz) dripping or butter
1 quantity puff pastry (page 180)
1 egg, lightly beaten

To make the pâté, melt half the butter in a frying pan. Add the shallots and garlic and cook until softened but not browned.

Preheat the oven to 220°C (425°F/Gas 7). Remove any discoloured spots from the chicken livers, wash and pat dry. Sauté the livers in the frying pan for 4–5 minutes, or until cooked but still a little pink in the centre. Cool completely, then process in a food processor with the rest of the butter and the brandy. Alternatively, chop the livers, push through a sieve and mix with the butter and brandy. Season.

Tie the beef four or five times along its length to keep it in shape. Heat the dripping in a roasting tin and brown the beef on all sides, then roast for

20 minutes. Allow to cool and remove the string. Reduce the oven to 200°C (400°F/ Gas 6).

Roll the pastry into a rectangle to cover the beef fillet completely. Trim the edges and keep them for decoration. Spread the pâté over the pastry, leaving a border. Brush the border with beaten egg.

Lay the fillet on the pastry and wrap it up tightly like a parcel, pressing the seams together firmly and tucking the ends under. Put the parcel, seam-side down, on a baking tray and brush all over with egg. Cut the trimmings to decorate the pastry and brush with egg. Bake for 25–30 minutes for rare and 35–40 minutes for medium. Allow the beef to rest for 5 minutes before carving.

SERVES 6

Far left: Spread the pâté over the pastry, leaving a border around the edge.

Left: Fold the beef tightly into the pastry parcel as the meat will shrink slightly when cooked.

Paupiettes de veau
Veal Paupiettes

STUFFING
30 g (1 oz) butter
2 French shallots, finely chopped
1 garlic clove, crushed
200 g (7 oz) minced (ground) pork
200 g (7 oz) minced (ground) veal
1 egg
2 tablespoons dry white wine
3 tablespoons fresh white breadcrumbs
2 tablespoons finely chopped parsley

4 x 150 g (6 oz) veal escalopes, pounded flat

SAUCE
30 g (1 oz) clarified butter
1 onion, diced
1 carrot, diced
1 celery stalk, diced
80 ml (3 fl oz/⅓ cup) white wine
2 teaspoons tomato paste (concentrated purée)
1 bay leaf
330 ml (12 fl oz/1⅓ cups) brown stock

To make the stuffing, melt the butter in a small saucepan and cook the shallots over gentle heat until softened but not browned. Add the garlic and cook for a further 2 minutes, then set aside to cool. Mix with the other stuffing ingredients and season with salt and pepper.

Lay the veal escalopes flat and spread with the stuffing, leaving a narrow border around the edge. Roll up the paupiettes, then tie up with string as you would a parcel.

To make the sauce, melt half the butter in a large sauté pan or frying pan. Add the onion, carrot and celery and cook over low heat until softened. Increase the heat and cook, stirring occasionally, until the vegetables are browned. Remove from the pan.

Heat the remaining clarified butter in the pan and brown the paupiettes, turning once. Remove from the pan, pour in the white wine and boil, stirring, for 30 seconds to deglaze the pan. Add the tomato paste and bay leaf.

Pour in the stock and bring to a simmer before adding the vegetables and paupiettes. Cover and cook for 12–15 minutes, or until a skewer poked into the centre of a paupiette comes out too hot to touch. Remove the paupiettes from the pan and keep warm.

Strain the sauce, pressing down on the vegetables with a spoon to extract as much liquid as possible. Return the sauce to the pan and boil until syrupy and reduced by half. Slice the paupiettes and serve with a little sauce poured over the top.

SERVES 4

Chapter 7

VEGETABLES

Regular visits to the fruit and vegetable markets play an integral part in the French way of life. There is an enduring appreciation of fresh produce, with recipes reflecting the very best that each season has to offer.

TIMBALES DE LÉGUMES
Vegetable Timbales

280 g (10 oz) carrots, chopped
280 g (10 oz) watercress, trimmed
280 g (10 oz) red capsicums (peppers)

185 ml (6 fl oz/³/4 cup) thick (double/heavy) cream
7 egg yolks
pinch of nutmeg

Steam the carrot until soft. Wash the watercress and put in a saucepan with just the water clinging to the leaves. Cover and steam for 2 minutes, or until the watercress is just wilted. Drain, cool and squeeze dry with your hands.

Preheat the grill (broiler). Cut the capsicums in half, remove the seeds and membrane and place, skin-side up, under the hot grill until the skin blackens and blisters. Cool before peeling away the skin.

Preheat the oven to 160°C (315°F/Gas 2–3). Purée each of the vegetables individually in a food processor, adding a third of the cream to the carrot to make a smooth purée. Pour the capsicum purée into a saucepan and stir over moderate heat until thickened. Put each purée in its own bowl to cool, then divide the remaining cream between the capsicum and watercress purées.

Stir 2 egg yolks into each purée. Divide the last yolk between the watercress and capsicum purées. Season with salt, pepper and nutmeg.

Grease four timbale moulds. Divide the carrot purée among the moulds and smooth the surface. Spoon the watercress purée on top of the carrot purée and smooth the surface. Finish with the capsicum purée and smooth the surface.

Put the timbale moulds in a roasting tin and then add hot water to come halfway up the sides of the timbales. Cook in this bain-marie for 1¼ hours.

To serve, hold a plate on top of each timbale. Tip upside down, give the plate and timbale one sharp shake and the timbale will release itself. Serve the timbales with a salad and baguette.

SERVES 4

Far left: Stir the egg yolks into the cooled purées.

Left: Smooth each layer as you put it in the mould, so the timbale is neat and even when turned out.

CHOU VERT FARCI

Stuffed Green Cabbage

Chou vert farci is a traditional dish from the cooler regions of France – the cabbage can cope with a harsher climate than many other vegetables and in this dish it is padded out with meat to make a filling main course.

STUFFING

4 ripe tomatoes
50 g (2 oz/⅓ cup) pine nuts
500 g (1 lb 2 oz) pork sausagemeat
150 g (6 oz) streaky bacon, finely chopped
1 onion, finely chopped
2 garlic cloves, crushed
160 g (6 oz/2 cups) fresh breadcrumbs
2 eggs
1 tablespoon mixed herbs

1 savoy cabbage, or other loose-leafed cabbage
lemon juice

BRAISING LIQUID

30 g (1 oz) butter
2 French shallots, chopped
1 large carrot, chopped
1 celery stalk, chopped
1 potato, diced
80 ml (3 fl oz/⅓ cup) medium-dry white wine
250 ml (9 fl oz/1 cup) chicken stock

To make the stuffing, score a cross in the top of each tomato, plunge them into boiling water for 20 seconds and then peel the skin away from the cross. Chop finely, discarding the cores.

Toast the pine nuts under a hot grill (broiler) for 2–3 minutes until lightly browned. Mix together all the stuffing ingredients and season.

Carefully separate the cabbage leaves, trying not to tear them. Save the cabbage heart for use later. Bring a large pan of water to the boil, add a little lemon juice and blanch the cabbage leaves a few at a time. Refresh in cold water, then drain.

Spread out a damp tea towel (dish cloth) on the work surface. Place the four largest cabbage leaves in a circle on the cloth with the stems meeting in the middle and the leaves slightly overlapping each other. Spread some of the stuffing over the leaves as evenly as you can.

Arrange another four cabbage leaves on top and spread with more stuffing. Continue the layers with the remaining cabbage leaves and stuffing, finishing with the smallest leaves. Bring the sides of the tea towel up to meet each other, wrapping the cabbage in its original shape. Tie into a ball with string.

To make the braising liquid, melt the butter in a large casserole or saucepan and sauté the chopped vegetables for a couple of minutes. Add the wine and boil for 2 minutes, then add the chicken stock. Lower the cabbage into the liquid. Cover tightly and simmer for 1¼ hours, or until a metal skewer comes out too hot to touch when poked into the centre of the cabbage. Lift out, unwrap and drain on a wire rack for 5 minutes.

To serve, place some of the braising vegetables and liquid into shallow serving bowls. Top with a wedge of stuffed cabbage.

SERVES 6

Petits pois à la française

Peas with Onion and Lettuce

Lettuce is often thought of as purely a salad green, but in fact until the eighteenth century it was more usually cooked than raw, and in France it is still often eaten this way, particularly in this dish.

50 g (2 oz) butter
16 small pickling onions or French shallots
500 g (1 lb 2 oz) shelled fresh peas
250 g (9 oz) iceberg lettuce heart, finely shredded

2 sprigs of parsley
1 teaspoon caster (superfine) sugar
125 ml (4 fl oz/½ cup) chicken stock
1 tablespoon plain (all-purpose) flour

Melt 30 g (1 oz) of the butter in a large saucepan. Add the onions or shallots and cook, stirring, for 1 minute. Add the peas, shredded lettuce, parsley sprigs and sugar.

Pour in the chicken stock and stir well. Cover the pan and cook over moderately low heat, stirring a couple of times, for 15 minutes, or until the onions are cooked through. Remove the parsley.

Mix the remaining butter with the flour to make a beurre manié. Add small amounts to the vegetables, stirring until the juices thicken a little. Season well with salt and black pepper.

SERVES 6

GRATIN DAUPHINOIS
Creamy Scalloped Potatoes

There are a number of versions of this regional dish from Dauphiné, some without the topping of cheese. In fact, the word gratin originally referred not to the topping, but to the crispy bits at the bottom of the pan.

1 kg (2 lb 4 oz) floury potatoes
2 garlic cloves, crushed
65 g (2 oz/ ½ cup) grated Gruyère cheese

pinch of nutmeg
315 ml (11 fl oz/1 ¼ cups) thick (double/heavy) cream
125 ml (4 fl oz/ ½ cup) milk

Preheat the oven to 170°C (325°F/Gas 3). Thinly slice the potatoes with a mandolin or sharp knife. Butter a 23 x 16 cm (9 x 6½ in) ovenproof dish and layer the potatoes, sprinkling the garlic, grated cheese, nutmeg and seasoning between the layers and leaving a bit of cheese for the top.

Pour the cream and milk over the top and sprinkle with the cheese. Bake for 50–60 minutes, or until the potatoes are completely cooked and the liquid is absorbed. If the top browns too much, loosely cover it with foil. Set aside to rest for 10 minutes before serving.

SERVES 6

POMMES DE TERRE BOULANGÈRE
Boulangère Potatoes

1 kg (2 lb 4 oz) potatoes
1 large onion
2 tablespoons finely chopped parsley

500 ml (17 fl oz/2 cups) hot chicken or vegetable stock
25 g (1 oz) butter, cubed

Preheat the oven to 180°C (350°F/Gas 4). Thinly slice the potatoes and onion with a mandolin or sharp knife. Build up alternate layers of potato and onion in a 20 x 10 cm (8 x 4 in) deep ovenproof dish, sprinkling the parsley, salt and black pepper between each layer. Finish with a layer of potato. Pour the stock over the top and dot with butter.

Cover with foil and bake on the middle shelf of the oven for 30 minutes, then remove the foil and lightly press down on the potatoes to keep them submerged in the stock. Bake for 30 minutes, or until the potatoes are tender and the top is golden brown. Serve piping hot.

SERVES 6

CAROTTES À LA VICHY
Glazed Carrots with Parsley

500 g (1 lb 2 oz) carrots
1/2 teaspoon salt
1 1/2 teaspoons sugar

40 g (1 1/2 oz) butter
1 1/2 tablespoons chopped parsley

Thinly slice the carrots, then put in a deep frying pan. Cover with cold water, add the salt, sugar and butter and simmer until the water has evaporated.

Shake the pan to glaze the carrot, then add the parsley, toss together and serve.

SERVES 6

RATATOUILLE
Mediterranean Vegetable Stew

The name ratatouille comes from the French word for 'mix' and was previously used as a familiar term for any stew. This recipe follows the traditional version, with each ingredient being fried separately before the final simmering.

4 tomatoes
2 tablespoons olive oil
1 large onion, diced
1 red capsicum (pepper), diced
1 yellow capsicum (pepper), diced
1 eggplant (aubergine), diced
2 zucchini (courgettes), diced

1 teaspoon tomato paste (concentrated purée)
1/2 teaspoon sugar
1 bay leaf
3 sprigs of thyme
2 sprigs of basil
1 garlic clove, crushed
1 tablespoon chopped parsley

Score a cross in the top of each tomato, plunge them into boiling water for 20 seconds and then peel the skin away from the cross. Chop roughly.

Heat the oil in a frying pan over low heat. Add the onion and cook for 5 minutes. Add the capsicums and cook, stirring, for 4 minutes. Remove from the pan and set aside. Fry the eggplant until lightly browned all over and then remove from the pan.

Fry the zucchini until browned, and then return the onion, capsicums and eggplant to the pan. Stir in the tomato paste and cook for 2 minutes. Add the tomato, sugar, bay leaf, thyme and basil, stir well, cover and cook for 15 minutes. Remove the bay leaf, thyme and basil.

Mix together the garlic and parsley and add to the ratatouille at the last minute. Stir and serve.

SERVES 4

DESSERTS AND BAKING

French classic cuisine has established the benchmark by which all desserts and pâtisserie items are judged. Soufflés, brûlées, mousses, crêpes and tarts are among the exceptional array of divine and decadent sweets.

Soufflé aux framboises

Raspberry Soufflé

There is sometimes confusion about the difference between a soufflé and a mousse. Technically, a soufflé is hot and a mousse is cold. A mousse is held up by gelatine and egg white and won't collapse like a hot soufflé, which is held up by hot air.

40 g (1½ oz) unsalted butter, softened
170 g (6 oz/¾ cup) caster (superfine) sugar

SOUFFLE
½ quantity crème pâtissière (page 184)
400 g (14 oz) raspberries

3 tablespoons caster (superfine) sugar
8 egg whites
icing (confectioners') sugar

Brush a 1.5 litre (6 cup) soufflé dish with the soft butter. Pour in the caster sugar, turn the dish to coat thoroughly and then tip out any excess sugar. Preheat the oven to 190°C (375°F/Gas 5) and put a baking tray in the oven to heat up.

Warm the crème pâtissière in a heatproof bowl over a saucepan of simmering water, then remove from the heat. Purée the raspberries and half the sugar in a blender or food processor (or mix by hand). Pass through a fine nylon sieve to get rid of the raspberry seeds. Add the crème pâtissière to the puréed raspberries and whisk together.

Beat the egg whites in a clean dry bowl until firm peaks form. Gradually whisk in the remaining

caster sugar to make a stiff glossy mixture. Whisk half of the egg white into the raspberry mixture to loosen it and then use a large metal spoon to fold in the remainder. Pour into the soufflé dish and run your thumb around the inside rim of the dish, about 2 cm (¾ in) into the soufflé mixture, to help the soufflé rise without sticking.

Bake on the hot baking tray for 10–12 minutes, or until the soufflé is well risen and wobbles slightly when tapped. Test with a skewer through a crack in the side of the soufflé – the skewer should come out clean or slightly moist. If it is slightly moist, by the time you get the soufflé to the table, it will be cooked in the centre. Serve immediately, dusted with a little icing sugar.

SERVES 6

When adding beaten egg white to a mixture, whisk in a small amount first to loosen it. This allows you to fold in the rest without losing the volume.

Gâteau basque

Basque Tart

The Basque country is squeezed into the Southwestern corner of France, bordered by the sea on one side and Spain on the other. Just about every Basque household has its own recipe for the baked tart, which is also known as Véritable Pastiza.

ALMOND PASTRY

400 g (14 oz/3¼ cups) plain (all-purpose) flour
1 teaspoon finely grated lemon zest
55 g (2 oz/½ cup) ground almonds
145 g (5 oz/⅔ cup) caster (superfine) sugar
1 egg
1 egg yolk
¼ teaspoon natural vanilla extract
150 g (6 oz) unsalted butter, softened

ALMOND CRÈME PÂTISSIERE

6 egg yolks
200 g (7 oz) caster (superfine) sugar
60 g (2 oz/½ cup) plain (all-purpose) flour
55 g (2 oz/½ cup) ground almonds
1 litre (35 fl oz/4 cups) milk
4 vanilla pods

4 tablespoons thick black cherry or plum jam (jelly)
1 egg, lightly beaten

To make the almond pastry, mix the flour, lemon zest and almonds together, tip onto a work surface and make a well in the centre. Put the sugar, egg, egg yolk, vanilla extract and butter in the well.

Mix together the sugar, eggs and butter, using a pecking action with your fingertips and thumb. Once they are combined, use the edge of a palette knife to incorporate the flour, flicking it onto the dough and chopping through it. Bring the dough together with your hands. Wrap in plastic wrap and put in the fridge for at least 30 minutes.

Roll out two-thirds of the almond pastry to fit a 25 cm (10 in) tart ring. Trim the edge and chill in the fridge for another 30 minutes. Preheat the oven to 180°C (350°F/Gas 4).

To make the crème pâtissière, whisk together the egg yolks and sugar until pale and creamy. Sift in the flour and almonds and mix together well.

Put the milk in a saucepan. Split the vanilla pods in two, scrape out the seeds and add the whole lot to the milk. Bring just to the boil and then strain over the egg yolk mixture, stirring continuously. Pour the mixture back into the clean saucepan and bring to the boil, stirring constantly – it will be lumpy at first but will become smooth as you stir. Boil for 2 minutes, then leave to cool.

Spread the jam over the base of the pastry case, then spread with the crème pâtissière. Roll out the rest of the pastry to make a top for the pie. Brush the edge of the pastry case with the beaten egg, put the pastry top over it and then press together around the side. Trim the edge. Brush the top of the pie with the beaten egg and gently score in a crisscross pattern. Bake for 40 minutes, or until golden brown. Cool for at least 30 minutes before serving, either slightly warm or cold.

SERVES 8

Madeleines
Madeleines

3 eggs
115 g (4 oz/$\frac{1}{2}$ cup) caster (superfine) sugar
155 g (6 oz/1 $\frac{1}{4}$ cups) plain (all-purpose) flour

100 g (4 oz) unsalted butter, melted
grated zest of 1 lemon and 1 orange

Preheat the oven to 200°C (400°F/Gas 6). Brush a tray of madeleine moulds with melted butter and coat with flour, then tap the tray to remove the excess flour.

Whisk the eggs and sugar until the mixture is thick and pale and the whisk leaves a trail when lifted. Gently fold in the flour, then the melted butter and grated lemon and orange zest. Spoon into the moulds, leaving a little room for rising. Bake for 12 minutes (small madeleines will only need 7 minutes), or until the madeleines are very lightly golden and springy to the touch. Remove from the tray and cool on a wire rack.

MAKES 14 (OR 30 SMALL ONES)

Clafoutis aux cerises
Cherry Clafoutis

It is traditional to leave the stones in the cherries when you make a clafoutis (they add a bitter almost-almond flavour during the cooking), but you'd better point this out when you're serving the pudding.

185 ml (6 fl oz/$^3/_4$ cup) thick (double/heavy) cream
1 vanilla pod
125 ml (4 fl oz/$^1/_2$ cup) milk
3 eggs
55 g (2 oz/$^1/_4$ cup) caster (superfine) sugar

85 g (3 oz/$^2/_3$ cup) plain (all-purpose) flour
1 tablespoon kirsch
450 g (1 lb) black cherries
icing (confectioners') sugar

Preheat the oven to 180°C (350°F/Gas 4). Put the cream in a small saucepan. Split the vanilla pod in half, scrape out the seeds and add the whole lot to the cream. Heat gently for a few minutes. Remove from the heat, add the milk and cool. Strain to remove the vanilla pod.

Whisk the eggs with the sugar and flour, then stir into the cream. Add the kirsch and black cherries and stir well. Pour the mixture into a 23 cm (9 in) round baking dish and bake for 30–35 minutes, or until golden. Dust with icing sugar and serve.

PICTURED LEFT

SERVES 6

PITHIVIERS
Almond Pastry

Originating in Pithiviers in the Loire Valley, this pastry is traditionally served on twelfth night, when it is known as Galette des Rois and usually contains a bean that brings good luck to whoever finds it in their slice.

FILLING
140 g (5 oz) unsalted butter, at room temperature
145 g (5 oz/²/₃ cup) caster (superfine) sugar
2 large eggs, lightly beaten
2 tablespoons dark rum
finely grated zest of 1 small orange or lemon

140 g (5 oz/1 ¹/₃ cups) ground almonds
1 tablespoon plain (all-purpose) flour

1 quantity puff pastry (page 180)
1 egg, lightly beaten
icing (confectioners') sugar

To make the filling, beat the butter and sugar until pale and creamy. Mix in the beaten eggs, little by little, beating well after each addition. Beat in the rum and the orange or lemon zest and then lightly fold in the almonds and flour. Put the filling in the fridge to firm a little while you roll out the pastry.

Cut the pastry in half and roll out one half. Cut out a 28 cm (11 in) circle. Place on a large baking tray lined with baking paper and spread the filling over the pastry, leaving a clear border of 2 cm (³/4 in) all the way round. Brush a little beaten egg over the border to help the pastry stick together.

Roll out the other half of the pastry and cut out a second circle the same size as the first. Lay this

circle on top of the filling. Firmly press the edges of the pastry together, cover and refrigerate for at least 1 hour (several hours or overnight is fine).

Preheat the oven to 220°C (425°F/Gas 7). Brush the top of the pie with the beaten egg to give it a shiny glaze. Be careful not to brush egg on the side of the pie or the layers won't rise properly. Working from the centre to the outside edge, score the top of the pithiviers with curved lines in a spiral.

Bake the pithiviers for 25–30 minutes, or until well risen and golden brown. Dust with icing sugar and allow to cool. Cut into slices to serve.

SERVES 6

Right: Leave a clear border around the filling, then brush it with beaten egg.

Far right: Place the second circle of pastry on top of the filling and press the two circles together.

Tarte Tatin

Tarte Tatin

This famous dessert is named after the Tatin sisters who ran a restaurant near Orléans at the beginning of the twentieth century. They certainly popularised the dish, but may not have invented it themselves.

1.5 kg (3 lb 6 oz) dessert apples
70 g (2 oz) unsalted butter
170 g (6 oz/³⁄₄ cup) caster (superfine) sugar
1 quantity tart pastry (page 178)

CRÈME CHANTILLY
185 ml (6 fl oz/³⁄₄ cup) thick (double/heavy) cream
1 teaspoon icing (confectioners') sugar
¹⁄₂ teaspoon natural vanilla extract

Peel, core and cut the apples into quarters. Put the butter and sugar into a deep 25 cm (10 in) frying pan with an ovenproof handle and heat until the butter and sugar have melted together. Arrange the apples tightly in the frying pan, making sure there are no gaps. You will be turning the tart out the other way up, so arrange the apple pieces so that they are neat underneath.

Cook over low heat for 35–40 minutes, or until the apple is soft, the caramel lightly browned and any excess liquid has evaporated. Baste the apple with a pastry brush every so often, so that the top is caramelised as well. Preheat the oven to 190°C (375°F/Gas 5).

Roll out the pastry on a lightly floured surface to a circle slightly larger than the frying pan and about 3 mm (¹⁄₈ in) thick. Lay the pastry over the apple and press down around the edge to enclose it completely. Trim the edge of the pastry and then fold the edge back on itself to give a neat finish.

Bake for 25–30 minutes, or until the pastry is golden and cooked. Remove from the oven and leave to rest for 5 minutes before turning out. (If any apple sticks to the pan, just push it back into the hole in the tart.)

To make the crème chantilly, put the cream, icing sugar and vanilla extract in a chilled bowl. Whisk until soft peaks form and then serve with the hot tarte tatin.

SERVES 8

Wedge the apple quarters tightly into the pan – they will shrink as they cook.

PÂTISSERIE

Pâtisserie, the art of cake and pastry making, is the most delightful and elaborate of culinary arts — the only one where beautiful decoration carries equal weight to the flavour of the food.

Pâtisserie can be traced back to the simple cakes of the ancient world and the pastry-making of the Middle-East, with its use of sugar, spices and nuts. From the Crusades onwards, these techniques and ingredients filtered into Europe and when in the sixteenth century Catherine de Medici and her retinue of Italian chefs arrived at the French court, they revolutionised French pâtisserie with their skills, such as the invention of choux pastry. In the early nineteenth century, Antonin Carême became the first of a line of great Parisian pâtissiers (pastry chefs). He was famous for his fantastic architectural creations, including croquembouches shaped into famous buildings.

Pâtisserie refers not only to the pastries, but also to the place where they are made and sold. Pâtisseries are sometimes solely shops, but often have a salon de thé attached where patrons can enjoy a pâtisserie in the mid-morning or afternoon, the favoured times for indulging in such a treat. Pâtisseries also sell candied fruits, chocolates and beautiful items to finish a meal or present as a gift. They display their pâtisserie elegantly, and the customers are presented with beautifully wrapped purchases.

Pastry making is one of France's most respected culinary arts, one that is even protected by its own patron saint, Saint Honoré. Pâtissiers can become members of professional organizations, such as The National Confederation of Pastry Chefs and the Relais Desserts International Professional Organization of Master Pastry Makers. One of the signs of these organizations hanging above a pâtisserie shows a real commitment to the trade.

Every region of France has its own pâtisserie specialities. In Alsace-Lorraine in the Northeast, there are Austrian-inspired Kugelhopf and strudels and wonderful fruit tarts, especially those that use Mirabelle plums. Paris is famed for its pâtisserie shops, and dark, bitter chocolate is a Northern speciality, especially in the cork-shaped bouchons from Champagne. In the Northwest, Brittany and Normandy's dairy farming and apples are used to create buttery Breton biscuits and the finest tarte aux pommes. In the East and Centre, Lyon is home to Bernachon, one of France's finest pâtisseries-confiseries, while pain d'épices, a spicy gingerbread, has been made in Dijon since the fifteenth century. The Southwest is known for its Basque cooking, which includes gâteau basque, as well as famous macarons from Saint Emilion and tarts made with Agen prunes. In the South there are candied fruit and marrons (chestnuts).

Paris-Brest

Paris-Brest

This large choux pastry cake was named after the Paris-Brest bicycle race. It was invented in 1891 by a canny Parisian pastry chef who owned a shop along the route and had the idea of producing these bicycle wheel-shaped cakes.

1 quantity choux pastry (page 179)
1 egg, lightly beaten
1 tablespoon flaked almonds
1 quantity crème pâtissière (page 184)
icing (confectioners') sugar

PRALINE
115 g (4 oz/½ cup) caster (superfine) sugar
90 g (3 oz/1 cup) flaked almonds

Preheat the oven to 200°C (400°F/Gas 6). Draw a 20 cm (8 in) circle on a piece of baking paper in pen so the circle shows through on the other side. Put the paper on a baking tray, pen-side down.

Put the choux pastry in a piping bag fitted with a nozzle about 2 cm (¾ in) wide. Pipe a ring of pastry over the guide you have drawn. Pipe another ring of pastry directly inside the first one to make one thick ring. Pipe another two circles on top of the first two and continue until all the choux pastry has been used. Brush the choux ring with beaten egg and sprinkle with the flaked almonds.

Bake the choux ring for 20–30 minutes, reduce the oven to 180°C (350°F/Gas 4) and then bake for a further 20–25 minutes. Transfer onto a wire rack.

Immediately slice the ring in half horizontally, making the base twice as deep as the top. Lift off the top and scoop out any uncooked pastry from the base. Leave to cool completely.

To make the praline, place a greased sheet of foil on the work surface. Put the sugar in a small pan with 125 ml (4 fl oz/½ cup) water and heat gently until completely dissolved. Bring to the boil and cook until deep golden. Quickly tip in the almonds and pour onto the foil. Spread a little and leave to cool. When the praline is hard, use a food processor or mortar and pestle to grind it to a fine powder.

Mix the praline into the cold crème pâtissière. Spoon into the base of the choux pastry ring and cover with the top. Dust with icing sugar to serve.

SERVES 6

Pipe a double thickness ring of choux pastry over the guide.

ÎLE FLOTTANTE
Floating Island

This round island of meringue floating on a sea of custard is often confused with another French meringue dessert, Oeufs à la neige. 'Floating island' is one large baked meringue, while 'eggs in the snow' are small poached meringues on custard.

MERINGUE
4 egg whites
125 g (5 oz/½ cup) caster (superfine) sugar
¼ teaspoon natural vanilla extract

PRALINE
55 g (2 oz/¼ cup) sugar
55 g (2 oz) flaked almonds

2 quantities crème anglaise (page 184)

Preheat the oven to 140°C (275°F/Gas 1). Heat a roasting tin in the oven. Grease and line the base of a 1.5 litre (52 fl oz/6 cup) charlotte mould with greaseproof paper. Lightly grease the base and side.

To make the meringue, beat the egg whites in a clean dry bowl until very stiff peaks form. Whisk in the sugar gradually to make a very stiff glossy meringue. Whisk in the vanilla extract.

Spoon the meringue into the mould, smooth the surface and place a greased circle of greaseproof paper on top. Put the mould into the hot roasting tin and pour boiling water into the tin to come halfway up the side of the charlotte mould. Bake for 50–60 minutes, or until a knife poked into the centre of the meringue comes out clean.

Remove the circle of paper, put a plate over the meringue and turn it over. Lift off the mould and the other circle of paper and leave to cool.

To make the praline, grease a sheet of foil and lay it out flat on the work surface. Put the sugar in a small saucepan with 3 tablespoons water and heat gently until completely dissolved. Bring to the boil and cook until deep golden, then quickly tip in the almonds and pour the mixture onto the oiled foil. Spread a little and leave to cool. When the praline has hardened, grind it to a fine powder in a food processor or with a mortar and pestle.

Sprinkle the praline over the meringue and pour a sea of warm crème anglaise around its base. Serve in wedges with the remaining crème anglaise.

SERVES 6

Grease and line the charlotte mould and place greased paper over the top after filling so that the meringue will not stick.

SOUFFLÉS AU CHOCOLAT

Chocolate Soufflés

Soufflés are renowned for their difficulty to make, but can in fact be very easy. If you are feeling particularly decadent when you serve these chocolate soufflés, make a hole in the top of each one and pour in a little cream.

40 g (1 ½ oz) unsalted butter, softened
170 g (6 oz/¾ cup) caster (superfine) sugar

SOUFFLÉS
1 quantity crème pâtissière (page 184)
90 g (3 oz/¾ cup) unsweetened cocoa powder

3 tablespoons chocolate or coffee liqueur
85 g (3 oz) dark chocolate, chopped
12 egg whites
3 tablespoons caster (superfine) sugar
icing (confectioners') sugar

Brush eight 315 ml (11 fl oz/1¼ cup) soufflé dishes with the soft butter. Pour a little caster sugar into each one, turn the dishes round to coat thoroughly and then tip out any excess sugar. Preheat the oven to 190°C (375°F/Gas 5) and put a large baking tray in the oven to heat up.

Warm the crème pâtissière in a bowl over a pan of simmering water, then remove from the heat. Whisk the cocoa powder, chocolate liqueur and chocolate into the crème pâtissière.

Beat the egg whites in a clean dry bowl until firm peaks form. Whisk in the sugar gradually to make a stiff glossy mixture. Whisk half the egg white into the crème pâtissière to loosen it, then fold in the remainder with a large metal spoon or spatula. Pour into the soufflé dishes and run your thumb around the inside rim of each dish, 2 cm (¾ in) into the soufflé mixture, to help the soufflés rise without sticking.

Put the soufflé dishes on the hot tray and bake for 15–18 minutes, or until the soufflés are well risen and wobble slightly. Test with a skewer inserted through a crack in the side of a soufflé – it should come out clean or slightly moist. If the skewer is slightly moist, by the time you get the soufflés to the table, they will be cooked in the centre. Serve immediately, dusted with a little icing sugar.

SERVES 8

Beat egg whites in a clean dry bowl – any hint of grease will prevent them aerating.

Tuiles
Tuiles

2 egg whites
55 g (2 oz/¼ cup) caster (superfine) sugar
15 g (½ oz) plain (all-purpose) flour

55 g (2 oz/½ cup) ground almonds
2 teaspoons peanut oil

Preheat the oven to 200°C (400°F/Gas 6). Line a baking tray with baking paper. Beat the egg whites in a clean dry bowl until slightly frothy. Mix in the sugar, then the flour, ground almonds and oil.

Place one heaped teaspoon of mixture on the tray and use the back of the spoon to spread it into a thin round. Cover the tray with tuiles, leaving 2 cm (¾ in) between them for spreading during cooking.

Bake for 5–6 minutes, or until the tuiles are lightly golden. Lift off the tray with a metal spatula and drape over a rolling pin while still warm to make them curl (you can use bottles and glasses as well). Cool while you cook the rest of the tuiles. Serve with ice creams and other creamy desserts.

MAKES 12

Tarte fine aux pommes
Apple Tart

1 quantity sweet pastry (page 179)
½ quantity crème pâtissière (page 184)

4 dessert apples
80 g (3 oz/¼ cup) apricot jam (jelly)

Preheat the oven to 180°C (350°F/Gas 4). Roll out the pastry to line a 23 cm (9 in) round loose-based fluted tart tin. Chill for 20 minutes.

Line the pastry shell with a crumpled piece of greaseproof paper and baking beads (use dried beans or rice if you don't have beads). Blind bake the pastry for 10 minutes, remove the paper and beads and bake for a further 3–5 minutes, or until the pastry is just cooked but still very pale.

Fill the pastry with the crème pâtissière. Peel and core the apples, cut them in half and then into thin slices. Arrange the apple slices over the top of the tart. Bake for 25–30 minutes, or until the apples are golden and the pastry is cooked. Set aside to cool completely.

Melt the apricot jam with 1 tablespoon water, then sieve out any lumps and brush over the apples to make them shine.

SERVES 8

Tarte Bourdaloue
Pear and Almond Tart

1 quantity sweet pastry (page 179)
55 g (2 oz/¼ cup) caster (superfine) sugar
1 vanilla pod
3 pears (ripe but still firm), peeled, halved and cored
3 tablespoons apricot jam (jelly)

ALMOND FILLING
150 g (6 oz) unsalted butter, softened
145 g (5 oz/⅔ cup) caster (superfine) sugar
few drops of natural vanilla extract
2 large eggs, lightly beaten
140 g (5 oz/1⅓ cups) ground almonds
finely grated zest of 1 small lemon
30 g (1 oz/¼ cup) plain (all-purpose) flour

Preheat the oven to 190°C (375°F/Gas 5). Roll out the pastry to line a 23 cm (9 in) round loose-based fluted tart tin. Chill for 20 minutes.

Put the sugar and vanilla pod in a saucepan. Add the pears and pour in just enough water to cover them, then remove the pears. Bring the water to a simmer and cook for 5 minutes. Add the pears, cover and poach for 5–10 minutes until tender. Drain and leave to cool.

To make the almond filling, beat the butter, sugar and vanilla extract together until pale and creamy. Beat in the eggs gradually and then fold in the almonds, lemon zest and flour.

Line the pastry shell with a crumpled piece of greaseproof paper and baking beads (use dried beans or rice if you don't have beads). Blind bake the pastry for 10 minutes, remove the paper and beads and bake for a further 3–5 minutes, or until the pastry is just cooked but still pale. Reduce the oven temperature to 180°C (350°F/Gas 4).

Spread three-quarters of the filling in the pastry shell and put the pear halves on top, cut-side down and stalk ends in the middle. Fill the gaps with the remaining filling. Bake for 35–40 minutes, or until the filling is golden and firm. Melt the apricot jam with 1 teaspoon water, sieve out any lumps and brush over the pears to make them shine.

SERVES 8

Right: Arrange the pears cut-side down in the pastry shell with the stalks pointing to the centre.

Far right: Fill the gaps between the pears with more of the almond filling.

BASICS

*An important step in mastering any cuisine is learning
the basic recipes and techniques. Straight from the recipe journal,
here are the ones no French cook would be without.*

Pâte à pain

Bread Dough

Lunch on thick slices of this rustic bread with unsalted butter and a good cheese. This is a basic bread dough and is easily flavoured – you could add chopped walnuts, fresh herbs, olives or cheese.

2 teaspoons dried yeast or 15 g (½ oz) fresh yeast
250 g (9 oz/2 cups) strong plain (all-purpose) flour

3 tablespoons olive oil
½ teaspoon salt

Mix the yeast with 125 ml (4 fl oz/½ cup) warm water. Leave for 10 minutes in a warm place until the yeast becomes frothy. If it does not bubble and foam in this time, throw it away and start again.

Sift the flour into a large bowl. Add the olive oil, salt and the yeast mixture. Mix until the dough clumps together and forms a ball.

Turn out onto a lightly floured surface. Knead the dough, adding a little more flour or a few drops of warm water if necessary, until you have a soft dough that is not sticky but is dry to the touch. Knead for 10 minutes, or until smooth, and the impression made by a finger springs back immediately.

Rub the inside of a large bowl with olive oil. Roll the ball of dough around in the bowl to coat with

oil, then cut a shallow cross on the top of the ball with a sharp knife. Leave the dough in the bowl, cover with a tea towel or put in a plastic bag and leave in a draught-free spot for 1–1½ hours, or until the dough has doubled in size (or leave in the fridge for 8 hours to rise slowly).

Knock back the dough by punching it with your fist several times to expel the air and then knead it again for a couple of minutes. (At this stage the dough can be stored in the fridge for 4 hours, or frozen. Bring back to room temperature before continuing.) Leave in a warm place to rise until doubled in size. Place in a tin, on a baking tray or use as directed in the recipe, then bake at 230°C (450°F/Gas 8) for 30 minutes. When cooked, the base of the bread will sound hollow when tapped.

MAKES 1 LOAF

Far left: Use flour that is packaged as 'strong' or 'bread' flour. You can use plain (all-purpose) flour or a mixture of plain and wholemeal, but the results won't be as good.

Left: Knock down the bread dough by punching it with your fist several times.

BRIOCHE

Brioche

Brioche is so buttery that you can serve it up for breakfast with nothing more fancy than a little good-quality jam (jelly) or curd. If you have one, use a fluted brioche tin, if not, an ordinary loaf tin will be fine.

2 teaspoons dried yeast or 15 g (1/2 oz) fresh yeast
60 ml (2 fl oz/1/4 cup) warm milk
2 tablespoons caster (superfine) sugar
220 g (8 oz/1 3/4 cups) plain (all-purpose) flour
pinch of salt

2 large eggs, lightly beaten
few drops natural vanilla extract
75 g (3 oz) butter, cubed
lightly beaten egg, to glaze

Mix the yeast with the warm milk and 1 teaspoon of the sugar. Leave for 10 minutes in a warm place until the yeast becomes frothy. If it does not bubble and foam in this time, throw it away and start again.

Sift the flour into a large bowl. Sprinkle with the salt and the rest of the sugar, then make a well in the centre and add the eggs, vanilla extract and yeast mixture. Use a wooden spoon to mix all the ingredients together, then use your hands to knead the dough for 1 minute to bring it together.

Transfer the dough to a lightly floured surface and gradually knead in the butter, piece by piece. Knead for 5 minutes, then put the dough in a clean bowl and cover with oiled plastic wrap. Leave to rise in a draught-free spot for 1–1 1/2 hours, or until the dough has doubled in size.

Knock back the dough by punching it with your fist several times to expel the air, and then lightly knead it again for a couple of minutes.

Shape the dough into a rectangle and place in a 20 x 7 x 9 cm (8 x 2 3/4 x 3 1/2 in) buttered loaf tin. Cover with oiled plastic wrap and leave to rise in a draught-free spot for 30–35 minutes, or until it has risen almost to the top of the tin. Preheat the oven to 200°C (400°F/Gas 6).

Once the brioche has risen, use a pair of scissors to carefully snip into the top of the dough at regular intervals. Snip three times on each side and twice at each end. The cuts should only be about 2.5 cm (1 in) deep. Brush the top with egg and bake for 30–35 minutes, or until the top of the brioche is rich brown. Turn the hot brioche out of the tin and tap the bottom of the loaf – if it sounds hollow, it is cooked. Put the brioche back in the tin upside down and return to the oven for 5 minutes to crisp the base of the loaf. Transfer to a wire rack and leave to cool.

MAKES 1 LOAF

CRÊPES
Crêpes

250 g (9 oz/2 cups) plain (all-purpose) flour
pinch of salt
1 teaspoon sugar
2 eggs, lightly beaten

410 ml (14 fl oz/1²/₃ cups) milk
1 tablespoon melted butter
butter or oil, for frying

Sift the flour, salt and sugar into a bowl and make a well in the centre. Mix the eggs and milk with 125 ml (4 fl oz/½ cup) water and pour slowly into the well, whisking all the time to incorporate the flour and make a smooth batter. Stir in the melted butter. Cover and refrigerate for 20 minutes.

Heat a crêpe pan or a deep non-stick frying pan and grease with a little butter or oil. Pour in enough batter to coat the base of the pan in a thin even layer and tip out any excess. Cook over moderate heat for 1 minute, or until the crêpe starts to come away from the side of the pan. Turn the crêpe and cook on the other side for 1 minute, or until lightly golden. Stack the crêpes on a plate with pieces of greaseproof paper between them and cover with foil while you cook the rest of the batter.

MAKES 12 SMALL OR 6 LARGE CREPES

PÂTE BRISÉE À L'OEUF
Tart Pastry

220 g (8 oz/1³/₄ cups) plain (all-purpose) flour
pinch of salt

150 g (6 oz) unsalted butter, chilled and diced
1 egg yolk

Sift the flour and salt into a large bowl. Add the diced butter and rub in with your fingertips until the mixture resembles breadcrumbs. Add the egg yolk and a little cold water (about 2–3 teaspoons) and mix with a palette knife until the dough just starts to come together. Bring the dough together with your hands and shape into a ball. Wrap in plastic wrap and put in the fridge to rest for at least 30 minutes. (You can also make the dough in a food processor, using the pulse button.)

Roll out the pastry into a circle on a lightly floured surface and use to line a tart tin, as directed in the recipe. Trim the edge and pinch up the pastry edge to make an even border raised slightly above the rim of the tin. Slide the tin onto a baking tray and rest in the fridge for 10 minutes.

MAKES 450 G (1 LB)

Pâte sucrée
Sweet Pastry

340 g (12 oz/2¾ cups) plain (all-purpose) flour
small pinch of salt
150 g (6 oz) unsalted butter

90 g (3 oz/¾ cup) icing (confectioners') sugar
2 eggs, beaten

Sift the flour and salt onto a clean work surface and make a well in the centre. Put the butter in the well and work, using a pecking action with your fingertips and thumb, until it is very soft. Add the sugar to the butter and mix together, then add the eggs and mix together.

Gradually incorporate the flour, flicking it onto the mixture and then chopping through it until you have a rough dough. Bring it together with your hands and then knead a few times to make a smooth dough. Roll into a ball, wrap in plastic wrap and put in the fridge for at least 1 hour.

Roll out the pastry into a circle on a lightly floured surface and use to line a tart tin, as directed in the recipe. Trim the edge and pinch up the pastry edge to make an even border raised slightly above the rim of the tin. Slide the tin onto a baking tray and rest in the fridge for 10 minutes.

MAKES 700 G (1 LB 9 OZ)

Pâte à choux
Choux Pastry

150 g (6 oz) unsalted butter
220 g (8 oz/1¾ cups) plain (all-purpose) flour,
   sifted twice

pinch of salt
7 eggs
1 tablespoon caster (superfine) sugar

Melt the butter with 375 ml (13 fl oz/1½ cups) water in a saucepan, then bring it to a rolling boil. Remove from the heat. Add the flour all at once and add the pinch of salt. Return to the heat and beat continuously with a wooden spoon to make a smooth shiny paste that comes away from the side of the pan. Cool for a few minutes.

Beat in the eggs one at a time, until shiny and smooth – the mixture should drop off the spoon but not be too runny. Beat in the sugar. Store in a pastry bag in the fridge for up to 2 days.

MAKES 500 G (1 LB 2 OZ)

Vinaigrette
Vinaigrette

1 garlic clove, crushed
½ teaspoon Dijon mustard

1 ½ tablespoons white wine vinegar
80 ml (3 fl oz/⅓ cup) olive oil

Mix together the garlic, mustard and vinegar. Add the oil in a thin stream, whisking continuously to form an emulsion. Season with salt and pepper.

Store in a screw-top jar in the fridge and shake well before use. You can also add some chopped herbs such as chives or chervil.

MAKES 125 ML (4 FL OZ/½ CUP)

Mayonnaise
Mayonnaise

4 egg yolks
½ teaspoon white wine vinegar

1 teaspoon lemon juice
500 ml (17 fl oz/2 cups) peanut oil

Put the egg yolks, vinegar and lemon juice in a bowl or food processor and whisk or mix until light and creamy. Add the oil, drop by drop from the tip of a teaspoon, mixing constantly until the mixture begins to thicken, then add the oil in a very thin stream. (If you're using a processor, pour in the oil in a thin stream with the motor running.) Season well.

MAKES 500 ML (17 FL OZ/2 CUPS)

Sauce béchamel
Béchamel Sauce

100 g (4 oz) butter
1 onion, finely chopped
90 g (3 oz/$^3/_4$ cup) plain (all-purpose) flour

1 litre (35 fl oz/4 cups) milk
pinch of nutmeg
bouquet garni

Melt the butter in a saucepan, add the onion and cook, stirring, for 3 minutes. Stir in the flour to make a roux and cook, stirring, for 3 minutes over low heat without allowing the roux to brown.

Remove from the heat and add the milk gradually, stirring after each addition until smooth.

Return to the heat, add the nutmeg and bouquet garni and cook for 5 minutes. Strain the hot sauce through a fine sieve into a clean pan. Lay a piece of buttered baking paper on the surface to prevent a skin forming.

MAKES 750 ML (27 FL OZ/3 CUPS)

Sauce velouté
Velvety Sauce

70 g (2 oz) butter
80 g (3 oz/$^2/_3$ cup) plain (all-purpose) flour

1 litre (35 fl oz/4 cups) hot chicken stock

Melt the butter in a saucepan. Stir in the flour to make a roux and cook, stirring, for 3 minutes over low heat without allowing the roux to brown. Cool to room temperature.

Add the hot stock and mix well. Return to the heat and simmer very gently for 10 minutes, or until thick. Strain the sauce through a fine sieve, cover and refrigerate until needed.

MAKES 500 ML (17 FL OZ/2 CUPS)

CRÈME ANGLAISE
Rich Custard Sauce

310 ml (11 fl oz/1¼ cups) milk
1 vanilla pod

2 egg yolks
2 tablespoons caster (superfine) sugar

Put the milk in a saucepan. Split the vanilla pod in half, scrape out the seeds and add the whole lot to the pan. (This will leave small black spots in the custard. If you don't want them, leave the vanilla pod whole.) Bring just to the boil. Whisk the egg yolks and sugar until light and fluffy. Strain the milk over the egg mixture, whisking constantly.

Pour the custard back into the saucepan and cook, stirring, until it is thick enough to coat the back of a wooden spoon. Do not let it boil or the custard will split. Strain into a clean bowl, lay plastic wrap on the surface to prevent a skin forming and refrigerate for up to 2 days.

MAKES 310 ML (11 FL OZ/1¼ CUPS)

CRÈME PÂTISSIÈRE
Pastry Cream

6 egg yolks
115 g (4 oz/½ cup) caster (superfine) sugar
30 g (1 oz/¼ cup) cornflour (cornstarch)
10 g (½ oz) plain (all-purpose) flour

560 ml (19 fl oz/2¼ cups) milk
1 vanilla pod
15 g (½ oz) butter

Whisk together the egg yolks and half the sugar until pale and creamy. Sift in the cornflour and flour and mix together well.

Put the milk, remaining sugar and vanilla pod in a saucepan. Bring just to the boil and then strain over the egg yolk mixture, stirring continuously.

Pour back into a clean saucepan and bring to the boil, stirring constantly. It will be lumpy at first but will become smooth as you stir. Boil for 2 minutes, then stir in the butter and leave to cool. Transfer to a bowl, lay plastic wrap on the surface to prevent a skin forming and refrigerate for up to 2 days.

MAKES 500 G (1 LB 2 OZ)

GLOSSARY

ANDOUILLETTE A sausage made from pork or veal chitterlings or tripe. Andouillettes are usually grilled (broiled) and often served with mustard, potatoes or cabbage. Some have an outer layer of lard that melts as they cook.

BAIN-MARIE Literally a 'water bath' for gentle oven-cooking of delicate terrines and desserts. Usually the dish is placed in a larger roasting tin, which is half-filled with water.

BEURRE MANIÉ A paste made by mixing together butter and flour. Stirred into sauces at the end of cooking to thicken them.

BOUQUET GARNI A bundle of herbs that is used to flavour dishes. Made by tying sprigs of parsley, thyme, celery leaves and a bay leaf in either a piece of muslin or portion of leek.

BROWN STOCK Stock made from browned beef or veal bones. As beef and veal stock are usually interchangeable, the term 'brown stock' is used. The best commercial stocks come freshly made in tubs.

BUTTER Butter is flavoured both by the lactic fermentation of cream and the diet of the cows from whose milk it is made. Butter from the Alps and Normandy is high quality and has a sweet flavour. French butter tends not to be heavily salted, with the amount varying between regions. Use either salted or unsalted butter for savoury dishes, but unsalted in sweet recipes.

CAPERS The pickled flowers of the caper bush. They are available preserved in brine, vinegar or salt and should be rinsed well and squeezed dry before use.

CERVELAS A long, fat pork sausage, often flavoured with garlic, pistachios or truffles. It is a boiling sausage (saucisse à cuire) and should be poached before browning under the grill (broiler). Ordinary pork sausages flavoured with pistachios can be used if cervelas are unavailable.

CHIPOLATA In Britain, chipolata means any small sausage. In France, however, a chipolata can be as long as an ordinary sausage but is always much thinner. Usually made from pork and pork fat, chipolatas are used as a garnish in French cooking.

CLARIFIED BUTTER Made by melting butter so that the fat separates out from the impurities and water. The fat is then either spooned off or the water tipped away and the butter reset. Clarified butter keeps for longer than ordinary butter because all the water has been removed. It can be used for cooking at high temperatures because it has a higher burning point.

CONFIT From the French word for 'preserve', confit is usually made from goose or duck meat, cooked in its own fat and then preserved in a jar or pot. It is eaten on its own or added to dishes such as cassoulet for extra flavour.

CORNICHON The French term for a small gherkin. If you can't find cornichons, you can use cocktail gherkins instead.

COURT BOUILLON A flavoured poaching liquid, usually for cooking fish.

CRÈME DE CASSIS Originating near Dijon in Burgundy, crème de cassis is a blackcurrant liqueur used in desserts.

CRÈME FRAÎCHE Often used in place of cream in the French kitchen. Lightly fermented, it has a slightly tart taste. Crème fraîche from Isigny has AOC status.

CURD CHEESE A smooth soft cheese made from curds that have not undergone lactic fermentation. Curd cheese is lower in fat than cream cheese, higher in fat than cottage cheese.

DIJON MUSTARD A pale yellow mustard, made from verjuice or white wine and mustard seeds that have been ground to a flour. Originally made in Dijon, this style of mustard is now made all over France.

FOIE GRAS The enlarged livers of fattened geese or ducks. It is regarded as a delicacy, with foie gras from Strasbourg and Southwest France both highly regarded.

FROMAGE FRAIS A fresh white cheese with a smooth creamy consistency. There are a number of varieties, many artisan-produced. Fromage blanc is traditionally used in Lyon's cervelle de canut. The fat content varies, which may affect its cooking qualities, but generally it makes a good low-fat alternative to cream.

GOOSE FAT A soft fat that melts at a low temperature and is used a lot in the cooking of Southwest France to give a rich texture to dishes. Available in tins from butchers. Duck fat can be substituted, although it needs to be heated to a higher temperature.

GRUYÈRE A pressed hard cheese with a nutty flavour. French Gruyère is available as Gruyère de Comté, which can have large holes, and Gruyère de Beaufort, which has virtually no holes. French Gruyère has a different flavour to Swiss, but the two are interchangeable in recipes.

HARICOT BEANS The general French name for beans, though the term is also used to mean just a kind of small, dried bean. Dried haricot beans come in many different varieties, including cannellini (kidney-shaped beans), flageolet (white or pale green beans) and navy beans (used to make baked beans).

JULIENNE To cut a vegetable or citrus rind into short, thin 'julienne' strips. Vegetables used as a garnish are often julienned for decorative purposes and to ensure quick, even cooking.

JUNIPER BERRIES Blackish-purple berries with a resinous flavour. Used in stews and robust game dishes. Use the back of a knife to crush the berries lightly before use to release their flavour.

MADEIRA A fortified wine from the Portuguese island of Madeira. There are a number of different varieties, from sweet (Malmsey or Malvasia and Bual), to medium (Verdelho) and dry (Sercial).

MAROILLES A square soft cheese with an orange washed-rind and a strong smell but sweet flavour. As an alternative, use other washed-rind varieties, such as Livarot, or a cheese with a white moulded rind, such as Camembert.

MUSSELS Grown commercially around the coast of France on bouchots (poles) driven into mud flats or in beds in estuaries, mussels can be eaten raw but they are usually cooked in dishes such as moules marinière. French mussels have blue-black shells and vary slightly in size and flavour according to the waters in which they are grown.

OLIVE Grown all over the South of France, the main varieties of French olives include the green pointed Picholines, purple-black Nyons and the small black olives of Nice, used in traditional Niçoise cooking. Fresh green olives are available from the summer and are picked before they start to turn black, while fresh black olives are available from the autumn through winter. Though green and black olives have a different flavour, they can be used interchangeably.

OLIVE OIL Extra-virgin and virgin olive oils are pressed without heat or chemicals and are best used in simple uncooked dishes and for salads. Pure olive oil can be used for cooking or deep-frying. Olive oil is made in the South of France, and after picking the olives in the autumn, each year's new oil is available in the winter.

OYSTER Two main species of oysters are available in France. Huîtres plates are European oysters, or natives. They have a flat round shell and are better in the winter months when they are not spawning. Huîtres creuses are the more common Portuguese (or Pacific) oysters, with deep, bumpy and flaky shells. Fines de claires are oysters grown in water full of algae, giving them a green colour and a distinct, iodine flavour.

PUY LENTILS Tiny green lentils from Puy in Central France that are AOC graded. Puy lentils do not need to be presoaked and do not break down when cooked. They have a firm texture and go very well with both meat and fish.

SAFFRON The dried dark orange stigmas of a type of crocus flower, used to add aroma and flavour to food. Only a few threads are needed for each recipe as they are very pungent.

SAUCISSE À CUIRE A cooking, or specifically boiling, sausage that is usually larger than an ordinary sausage. Saucisses à cuire are poached, either as part of a dish such as choucroute garnie or just with red wine.

TOULOUSE SAUSAGE A general term for meaty pork grilling (broiling) sausages, usually sold in a coil.

TRUFFLES Considered a delicacy, truffles are a type of fungus and have an earthy smell. The black truffles found in France, specifically around Périgord, are often considered the best black truffles in the world. Truffles are best eaten fresh, but can also be preserved in jars. They only need to be used in small amounts for flavouring.

VANILLA EXTRACT Made by using alcohol to extract the vanilla flavour from beans. Not to be confused with artificial vanilla essence that is made with synthetic vanillin. Use sparingly.

INDEX

Published in 2016 by Murdoch Books, an imprint of Allen & Unwin

Murdoch Books Australia
83 Alexander Street
Crows Nest NSW 2065
Phone: +61 (0) 2 8425 0100
Fax: +61 (0) 2 9906 2218
www.murdochbooks.com.au
info@murdochbooks.com.au

Murdoch Books UK
Erico House, 6th Floor
93–99 Upper Richmond Road
Putney, London SW15 2TG
Phone: +44 (0) 20 8785 5995
www.murdochbooks.co.uk
info@murdochbooks.co.uk

For Corporate Orders & Custom Publishing contact Noel Hammond,
National Business Development Manager, Murdoch Books Australia

Series Design Manager: Sarah Odgers
Designer: Jacqueline Duncan
Photography: Chris L. Jones and Howard Shooter
Food styling: Mary Harris
Production Manager: Alex Gonzalez

A cataloguing-in-publication entry is available from the catalogue of
the National Library of Australia at nla.gov.au.

ISBN 978 1 743366608 Australia
ISBN 978 1 743366615 UK

A catalogue record for this book is available from the British Library.

Colour reproduction by Splitting Image, Clayton, Victoria.
Printed by 1010 Printing International, China.